# CAREER PLANNING
## FOR TEENS

*How to Understand Your Identity, Cultivate Your Skills, Find Your Dream Job, and Turn That Into a Successful Career*

**EMILY CARTER**

# TABLE OF CONTENTS

*Your Free Gift*. . . . . . . . . . . . . . . . . . . . . . . . . . . . . . . . . . . . . . . . . . . . . . v

*Introduction* . . . . . . . . . . . . . . . . . . . . . . . . . . . . . . . . . . . . . . . . . . . 1

Chapter 1: **Understanding Yourself**. . . . . . . . . . . . . . . . . . . . . . 9

Chapter 2: **Exploring Career Options** . . . . . . . . . . . . . . . . . . . .21

Chapter 3: **Developing Essential Skills** . . . . . . . . . . . . . . . . . 35

Chapter 4: **Seeking Guidance** . . . . . . . . . . . . . . . . . . . . . . . . . . 55

Chapter 5: **Planning for Education and Training** . . . . . . . . 65

Chapter 6: **Gaining Practical Experience** . . . . . . . . . . . . . . . 79

Chapter 7: **Making Informed Decisions** . . . . . . . . . . . . . . . . 93

Chapter 8: **Taking Action**. . . . . . . . . . . . . . . . . . . . . . . . . . . . . . 107

Chapter 9: **Transitioning to the World of Work** . . . . . . . . .123

*Conclusion* . . . . . . . . . . . . . . . . . . . . . . . . . . . . . . . . . . . . . . . . . . 137

*About The Author.* . . . . . . . . . . . . . . . . . . . . . . . . . . . . . . . . . . . 143

*References* . . . . . . . . . . . . . . . . . . . . . . . . . . . . . . . . . . . . . . . . . 145

# YOUR FREE GIFT

Having the right mindset is the key when it comes to achieving success in any area of your life. As a way of saying thank you for your purchase, I want to offer you my book *Unleashing Your Potential: A Teenager's Guide to Developing a Growth Mindset and Opening Your Path to Success* for completely FREE of charge.

To get instant access, just scan the QR-code below or go to: https://lifeskillbooks.com/career-planning-free-bonus

Inside the book, you will discover...

✧ The difference between a fixed and growth mindset, how your mindset impacts your personal growth and success, and why a growth mindset is the one you should adopt.

✧ Practical strategies to cultivate a growth mindset, from daily habits to overcoming obstacles.

✧ How to utilize a growth mindset to supercharge your academic and career success.

✧ And much more!

But wait, there's more to come...

In addition to the *Unleashing Your Potential* eBook, I want to give you two additional special bonuses:

# BONUS 1

*The Essential Summer Job Handbook:*
*The Teen's Guide to a Fun and Profitable Summer*

Inside this exciting guide, you will discover...

✧ The many benefits of having a summertime job, from earning extra cash to gaining valuable experience and skills that will set you up for success in the future.

- ✧ The different types of jobs available for teens at different ages, and how to market yourself effectively to potential employers.

- ✧ Practical tips for avoiding being taken advantage of, and advice on tax considerations that every working teen needs to know.

# BONUS 2

*Raising Teens With Confidence: 10 Exclusive Blog Posts on Parenting Teens*

   I know this sounds boring if you're a teen, and that's completely fine. But for you parents out there, these unreleased blog posts offer a great opportunity to learn some new effective ways of parenting your teen.

Inside this compilation, you will discover...

✧ Invaluable insights and practical tips on how to navigate the challenges of parenting teenagers, from setting boundaries and dealing with mood swings to managing serious issues like drink and drug use.

✧ How to pick your battles wisely and let go of the small stuff, while still maintaining a strong connection with your teen and encouraging them to open up to you.

✧ Effective strategies for getting your teen to help out more at home, and how to strike the right balance between being a supportive parent and allowing your teen to develop their independence.

If you want to really make a change in your life for the better and get ahead of 95% of other teens, make sure to scan the QR-code below or head to the web address below to gain instant access to your bonuses.

https://lifeskillbooks.com/career-planning-free-bonus

# INTRODUCTION

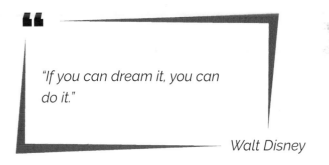

*"If you can dream it, you can do it."*

— *Walt Disney*

How many times have you looked at yourself in the mirror and thought, "What am I going to do with the rest of my life?"? Or how many times have you noticed your classmates and the people around you constantly working on themselves, leaving you feeling like you are falling behind? A certain level of panic might set in as you realize you don't have much time to prepare for the future. Fortunately, you can always turn that around – and today, you're starting to do just that!

The winds of change are coming as your secondary education ends. It is time to start thinking about career paths. As you walk through the halls of your high school, the terms career counseling and career planning become terms you meet more often. What does that mean? Do you suddenly have to think about tomorrow?

The short answer is yes. When you are a teenager, time is of the essence, and time waits for no one. Instead of starting to browse the options aimlessly, you took the logical first step and you purchased this book.

The importance of career planning during your teenage years will set the pace for how your career path will develop in the future. I am not saying that you can't thrive at a later age. However, during the crazy times of uncertainty that we live in, the best approach to the world of professional development is an early one. It is important to gain early access and exposure to help you achieve career awareness. But not only that. Through career planning in your teenage years, you enable a firmer and more harmonious career path that aligns with your wishes and goals.

Up until now, you may have used the classroom as an environment similar to the workplace. This is the perfect way to begin. It sets the tone for what you should expect in the future and helps you become more aware of your skills and interests. Nevertheless, it is still a classroom at the end of the day. It is still a closed and safe space where you can make mistakes and not be as involved as you should be.

This book can help you step out of your comfort zone. It can help you utilize the brainstorming bit and use it to your advantage. Once you take the first step, you will notice endless possibilities. The practices you get to learn and the experiences you are about to undergo will help create individualized access to a brighter tomorrow.

How does it sound so far? Convincing or not?

There is a second important aspect of choosing career planning during your teenage years, and it includes all the benefits you get from it.

Going through the process of choosing your career can help you identify your interests. It is okay if you weren't quite aware of your likes and dislikes up until now. This important aspect can help you choose the field that will make you happy in the future. Every person in the world has a "true calling," so why not figure out what yours is from an early age?

Another benefit you will gain is knowing how to make an informed decision. After all, there are all these factors to contribute; you might have difficulty navigating through it all. That is okay. That is what career advice is for. You can always rely on a mentor or a role model to help you get through the challenging period. Ultimately, they will motivate you and help you set goals that will lead you to a satisfying career option. Depending on the fields you are interested in, there is so much information to gather. Avoid losing yourself in the process. Understand the requirements, skills, and qualifications needed to succeed. Once you arm yourself with the appropriate knowledge, you will have all the power in the world!

But there is no knowledge without training, so surround yourself with the best options that can help you enhance everything you know. Training opportunities, volunteering opportunities, internships, shadowing people, and part-time jobs are all key points in your quest to thrive professionally. Consider this a two-way street – you get to advance your skills and learn many new ones, but you also get to identify the skills most employers require. I can teach you how to keep in mind all the future training that will act as a catalyst for your bright tomorrow!

Many of you have big dreams and want to achieve them but are scared of the outcome. Have no fear. All you need is to stay focused and keep working toward your goal. Considering everything, you will slowly start to enjoy the benefits of your careful career planning. Here are only a few of them to get you started:

 ✧ You will learn that this is your journey only. Being surrounded by adults, starting with your parents, teachers, relatives, counselors, etc., you might lose yourself. Starting to think that this is a decision that will affect anyone but you – meaning you need to take a step back. Instead, you will embed this in your brain – the journey is yours alone – enjoy it.

✧ There is a benefit to change. Change is something that will happen to you either way – why not take charge of it? Reading this book will give you exclusive insight into how to manage change and flourish every time you do it successfully.

✧ You will learn how to make mistakes and fix them as well. The decision-making process is the important part, but make no mistake about it, you will fail at it – at first. Every decision comes with the possibility of making a mistake. But every decision is also a valuable experience – you will teach yourself how to enjoy the good decisions and quickly fix the bad ones.

✧ You will learn how to make up your mind and if needed, to change it too. Career planning comes with a lot of twists and turns. You may start at one point with one goal in mind and end up in a completely different place. Your road to success will be filled with twists and turns and challenges wherever you look. It is essential to accept that, depending on everything you discover about yourself, you might need to change your plans (sometimes even completely).

✧ Keep learning – from everything. Every step you take comes with a lesson. The same goes for this book – every chapter is filled with lessons for you to remember. It all comes down to reinforcing your connection while seeking out new experiences.

✧ There is also always time to celebrate yourself. Don't forget to have fun while discovering everything you can about yourself. Above all, you are a teenager, and this is still your time to shine and have fun! Just remember to work hard during the process and celebrate every milestone you complete. This way, you will boost your confidence and maybe, some magic in the air!

Throughout this book, you will learn how to set up a system that works for you. The structure allows for being flexible and persistent and learning how to tackle every obstacle that comes your way. For starters, being true and honest with yourself is the best way to begin your journey toward professional success.

Other than that, I am also covering various topics such as how to explore career options and to broaden your horizons. Learning how to leap into the future by uncovering some potential job prospects that represent the future. But never stop working on yourself. Using your technical and transferable skills is a part of all job experiences – together, we will see how you can utilize them best.

It is not all about the technical part – you will also learn how to develop a fantastic support system filled with people you can trust. Allow me to enter a hidden part of your mind and explain the importance of role models. After doing that, you might realize you have had a role model all this time!

As the planning continues, you will also gain an understanding of what it means to have some practical experience before you dive head-first into the job world. I am covering all topics – from building the perfect portfolio and resume to successfully being a part of a job interview. Moving on, you get to discover how to recognize the available professional options. Weighing in the factors and knowing how to decide on your career is essential.

Once you understand how the market works, what types of job prospects are right there at your fingertips, and how to improve your skillset constantly, you will become an invaluable part of the force that drives the world.

Let me empower you to make an informed decision about your future. There is only one bridge between your dreams and reality, so take a walk with me. Today, we are commencing an amazing journey of career planning.

Today, your dreams are waiting – let's start chasing them together!

CHAPTER 1

# UNDERSTANDING YOURSELF

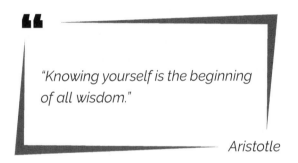

*"Knowing yourself is the beginning of all wisdom."*

*Aristotle*

Even though we live in a different era, this timeless truth continues to echo throughout the centuries.

But let's be honest for a moment – finding and understanding yourself can be incredibly tricky when you are a teenager. Driven by hormones and emotion, you wander through life's corridors while external factors try to sway you from your true self. And in this modern era, where the comparison to influential people can easily seduce you to build your interests around someone else's norms – the road can become even more challenging. Top it off with family expectations and other influences from your society, and voila; you are officially in the *"I don't know what I want"* maze. Oh, and the fact that so many career choices mount while you are already overwhelmed doesn't help either.

But how can you possibly get out of that maze and come face to face with your true self?

In short, the answer is within. You just need the right tools to guide you, which is what this chapter is all about. With self-assessment and personal reflection as your compass, you will uncover your inner landscape of interests, values, and skills. In addition, you will also learn how your personality traits play a major role in making the right career choice. By understanding who you are and where your interests and passions lie, you will not only define the first step toward your career but also unleash your full potential.

Now, prepare to see yourself from a different angle. Uncover the truth within, and relish how complex, unique, and beautiful you are.

## Self-Assessment and Personal Reflection

The first step towards choosing a career path that resonates with you is the act of self-assessing and reflecting. You need to be able to decide on something you will genuinely enjoy and be passionate about.

As a teenager, it is easy to be influenced and distracted by many external factors. That is why it is essential to simply find a quiet place, sit down, and think about all that makes you, YOU.

Let's start with your general values and motivations. Ask yourself, what truly matters to you? What do you value? Do you live and breathe in the name of a team spirit, or do you value a quieter and more individual approach? Is the support and presence of your family the motivation you need, or maybe you wish to become more independent and carve out your own path somewhere else? Are your relationships built on trust, and that kind of support motivates you to achieve any goal? Maybe accountability and responsibility are the pillars of your actions. Or maybe, you find that honesty and transparency are super important for progressing through life.

Whatever questions and thoughts arise, try to self-reflect and write it all down. Grab a piece of paper, a journal, or a notebook, and allow every answer to flow into it. I don't recommend typing on your phone or computer; a good old-fashioned piece of paper and a pen would do perfectly. This is because the writing process is slower on paper, and it allows you to savor every thought. It allows you time to think twice before you write something down – do you really want it or not? While composing your words, you will paint a visual image in your mind and have time to really mull things over. In addition, it is a fantastic exercise to gain clarity and open your path toward discovering yourself even further.

Only some things may be clear from the start, but by gradually working your way inwards, you will understand what shapes you as a person. Take a peek into the hidden nooks within – you just might be amazed at what you will find! Plus, by defining your values, you will gain the confidence you need to become empowered. After all, your beliefs are part of choosing a career path that reflects your principles. Slowly but surely, these principles will give you a purpose that will silence any external factor. Finally, you will see how a sketch of your persona emerges on what previously was a blank page. Trust me, as the days pass and you reflect more and more, that sketch will become more clearly defined.

The next step is to identify your talents, skills, and passions. It is the part called adding color to the sketch. But before you start pondering on that, I want you to throw aside any high expectations. Just forget about what you are supposed to be or what your society prefers. Even if you don't have the answers immediately, give yourself time. And let me assure you, not all talents revolve around being creative! You don't have to be a virtuoso to succeed in life. There is beauty and potential in everything.

That being said, in the next part, I will further help you narrow down your core values, identify your interests and skills, and even uncover some hidden talents just waiting to see the light of day.

# Identifying Your Values, Interests, and Skills

Through the part of self-discovery, you find out how to best utilize your interests and skills. However, you have to define them first before you can move any further. In this part, we will put focus on your self-discovery through immersing yourself in practical activities, revealing your interests, values, and skills.

## *Values*

Values are the pillar of every human being. A clear-cut set helps you define who you are, what your core values are, and how they help you shape yourself into a confident young person.

Values can even boost your decision-making skills. So, for the sake of your bright future, try to outline them.

Once you have your general values mapped out, it is time to dive into something more specific. As I already mentioned, what you stand for needs to be aligned with your career. You cannot be one person privately and someone entirely different when it comes to your professional progress. Not only will you be fooling yourself that it is what you want or need, but it will be draining to go against your values. Simply put, your career path should complement your personality rather than go the opposite way.

With the help of these questions, you will gain a clearer idea of what matters and motivates you the most:

✧ Is being a leader important to you? Or are you entirely okay doing your thing in the background?

✧ Are you comfortable working and expanding on someone else's ideas, or maybe you wish to cultivate and "grow" your own?

✧ Is creativity something you excel at and a big part of who you are?

✧ Are you someone who wants their actions to benefit society?

✧ Do you perform better when you have clearly defined rules or when you are free to experiment?

✧ Is gaining more knowledge a priority?

✧ Does being under pressure motivate you, or does it have a reverse effect?

✧ Do you wish to advance or thrive in your comfort zone?

For some of the questions, you might need more time to decide what to answer – which is normal! If you find yourself struggling to answer, you can do some of the interests below and then get back to answering these. Sometimes one aspect may fill in the blanks in the other.

### Interests

It goes without saying that your interests should also be aligned with your career. But this is also important in the long run – your career choice should be engaging and satisfying.

As a teenager, it is easy to indulge in many activities or have periods when you are entirely passive. That being said, it is not really easy to immediately think of everything that interests you. And that is perfectly okay because I have the solution for that too. Here is an interesting exercise you can do that can bring you a step closer to answering your question.

As you can see below, all you need to do is think of a few past and present experiences. Dive in!

*Think of experiences from your past:*

✧ List up to ten notable things that brought you some satisfaction, made you feel like you've accomplished something, or pushed you out of your comfort zone – in a challenging yet exciting and enjoyable way.

✧ Feel free to write one sentence that will explain why you found it satisfactory.

✧ Read them out loud and begin noticing some patterns.

*Think of current interests and activities (out of school):*

✧ Would you rather read or watch a movie? Or both?

✧ What are the genres that you enjoy the most?

✧ What was the theme of your most recent enjoyable conversation? Do you talk about that subject often, and how do you feel about it?

✧ Do you have a role model? If yes, who and why?

✧ What is your ultimate travel destination?

- ✧ What are the topics that often grab your attention – both during conversations and when watching the news?

- ✧ What entertains you the most?

- ✧ Do you feel like you are more of an outdoor or an indoor person?

- ✧ Whenever you had to choose between watching a documentary or playing a video game, which one captured your attention more?

- ✧ Have you noticed yourself unconsciously doing something (writing, drawing, or maybe playing guitar)? Is there a thing that so powerfully draws you in, you lost yourself in time and space?

Even though some of the questions may seem unrelated at this point, I promise each has its own purpose. Your favorite movie might not pass your exam or land you a job in the future, but it will open other doors like what your mind is drawn to, which genre, and how it relates to your life, etc. It provides a path towards introspective, creativity, expressing yourself, finding empathy, or maybe even confidence. Whatever you discover, it will benefit you in more ways than one.

## Skills

Last but not least, the part most teenagers dread – the skillset. Now, you might be terrified by the fact that you need to show a certain set of skills (even if it is only for yourself), that you freeze. That's okay! It is okay if your mind wanders aimlessly for a little while as you compose yourself. Give it a little bit of time, and then start doing this next exercise!

For this part, we will go over the activities and skills – to draw out potential hidden talents.

*Think of what kind of activities you enjoy and the skills that come with them:*

- ✧ List up to 10 activities you enjoyed. This can be absolutely anything!
- ✧ Next to each of those activities, write which technical skills you cultivated. These can be problem-solving, organizing, writing, narrating, debating, leading, helping with a specific aspect, etc.

Did you notice that you easily came up with your list of skills?

Every skill can be an arrow pushing you in the right direction. For example, if you are a good writer, this can serve you in multiple careers like publishing, journalism, teaching, book writing, etc. If you have a knack for solving challenging problems, your future can revolve around management and other areas like social jobs or politics. If you've always been good with numbers and technology, then your future area of expertise may be in the field of math, physics, technology, or something else along those lines! In essence, even a single skill can set the sails toward your ideal goals.

After finishing all three aspects, you will have plenty to think about. As you've never approached your goals from this perspective, you might also be surprised to rediscover your passions and interests. In essence, all of them will help you carve not only your career but also your overall future academic and job satisfaction. Moreover, some of them will reflect your personality traits, which is another factor to consider. All in all, they will help you fully shape yourself.

But how can you connect these traits to your professional life choices? If you can't quite make the connection yet, allow me to elaborate.

Take a look below at how they are important for navigating your way toward what you want and need.

## Personality Traits and Their Relevance to Career Choices

While your values, interests, and skills are essential to get an idea of your passions and abilities, your traits will complete the whole picture. Research shows that your future academic and job performance can be directly affected by your unique personality characteristics (Wille et al., 2010, 2012; Bakker et al., 2012). In a way, the better they complement one another, the more productive and happier you will be. For example, we can take the most general categorization of introverts and extroverts. You can easily see how an extrovert would fit in a career that revolves around being social, and an introvert would feel more comfortable doing something independently.

Simply put, by defining your traits, you can pinpoint your strengths and weaknesses, achieving better career satisfaction and maximizing your performance.

Where do you see yourself thriving the most? Naturally, you wouldn't be comfortable plunging into a career that doesn't align with your personality. No worries, I got you covered! If you need to know yourself better and highlight your personality traits, you need to look inward and do some work. For that reason, I suggest doing several tests such as the ones below. You can easily find each of them by doing a quick Google search:

- ✧ Myers-Briggs Type Indicator (MBTI) – This questionnaire is based on C.G. Jung's principles and shows the uniqueness of how your personality traits help you in your decision-making.

- ✧ The DISC test – This behavioral test dates back one century, and it was established by the psychologist William Moulton Marston. It represents four aspects: Dominance, Influence, Steadiness, and Compliance, which explain your day-to-day behavior and attitude toward others.

- ✧ The Hogan personality inventory (HPI) – I love this one as it describes the bright side of your personality. It basically shows your attitude toward others when you are at your best.

- ✧ Gallup's Clifton Strengths Assessment – Another amazing tool that will help you identify your emotions, thoughts, and how you behave. It is a fantastic way to discover your talents further.

✧ Enneagram Personality Test – Finally, we have the Enneagram, which will depict how you see the world and, naturally, how your emotions are shaped based on those horizons.

You can decide to do one, two, or all! If you feel like all would be too much for you, that's okay! Even getting one score can serve your purpose and enrich the journey to self-discovery and awareness.

I hope that you have started working on creating a better version of yourself because this is only the beginning! By working on this chapter's elements, you should have no difficulty doing the following:

✧ Self-assess your motivation and values and further reflect on them.

✧ Become inspired by your interests and skills.

✧ Acknowledge your personality traits and discover your strengths and weaknesses.

I believe that now that you have discovered so many things about yourself – both new and old – you feel excited to see where it can take you! From this point of view, yes, the possibilities are endless! So, without further ado, let's explore your career options in the following chapter.

## CHAPTER 2

# EXPLORING CAREER OPTIONS

> "At the center of your being, you have the answer; you know who you are, and you know what you want."
>
> — *Lao Tzu*

A s we move on together to the second chapter, there is no bigger truth than this.

You hold the power within to answer your most difficult questions. You know yourself best, and if you are honest with yourself, then you will start thriving! In this chapter, we tweak the saying from one of the greatest minds in the world – Lao Tzu, to fit our needs.

When exploring career options, it is natural to start thinking about two very important core questions; "Who am I?" and

"What is my life purpose?" Answering these two questions can help you get a step closer to getting the true sense of who you are.

Don't skip this step, as it is an important process to go through. As an individual teen, it can help you better understand yourself and your place in the world. At the moment, there must already be something that appeals to you more than anything else. That is a great starting point for you. As I guide you through some steps you can take, remember that the world is your oyster! The possibilities are endless, so keep an open mind.

## Broadening Horizons: Introducing a Wide Range of Career Paths

Broadening horizons or overcoming obstacles? Depends on how you look at it! It is natural for you to enjoy doing various things at your age. You may enjoy drawing, painting, writing, the news, insects, animals, technology, cakes – literally anything! At this stage, your future is bright and filled with adventures, so you first need to grasp that as a concept.

Broadening your horizons does not mean stepping into the uncomfortable but rather stepping out of your comfort zone by simply enhancing your best features. At your age, it is important to broaden your horizons and allow your opinion to change as many times as you need.

If you have been interested in, say, becoming a doctor as a young kid, that does not mean you need to keep following that path by any means necessary. Every once in a while, it is okay to stop and reflect on what you have done until now and how well you have developed.

This is where all your options come in. There is always a wide range of career paths for you to consider. In essence, broadening your horizons means growing and developing. For example, about 5 years have passed since you last said you wanted to be a doctor, and now, both your interests and perspective have shifted. You feel a little uncertain about your decision – many other driving forces pull you apart from medical school rather than push you closer.

During this period, you have developed some new skills and uncovered a few hidden talents that change everything. So then, why not change everything? Your speaking and listening skills have significantly improved, and you have sharpened your wit and are detail oriented. You started loving how society develops and want to be a part of changing it for the better. Law starts sounding like the better option with each passing day.

Here is where I empower you to go after what you want and after what your set of skills allows you to go after. There is no need to abandon your potential for anything just to complete the goal you (or your parents) set for yourself long ago.

The key is using your skills for something you will enjoy doing. Remember that your whole life is in front of you, and with a little bit of your help, it can unravel in the most magical of ways. Using the tips from the first chapter, outline the interests, values, and skills you are best at, and then take it from there!

Self-assessment is important. Ask yourself, "What do I enjoy the most?" – it is how you will identify the potential career paths that align with your personality and interests.

## Researching and Gathering Information on Different Industries and Professions

Next stop, you start your research! After you have collected the information about yourself, it is time to start implementing them. One of the most critical aspects of finding your true calling is looking into organizations and companies (even entire industries) and searching for someone with your specifications. Anything from thorough research on the internet to going to some networking events will do. Research allows you to thoroughly understand a potential professional path – requirements, expectations, and further developments.

This is how you identify career options and branches that perfectly fit you.

Also, think of it as an essential part of your journey toward becoming an adult. The time and resources you invest in this end up assisting you in choosing the right career prospect for you. So, set yourself up for a bright and happy future!

There are many ways you can begin pursuing the career that suits you the best. If you have never done research until now, have no fear! I'm equipping you with a complete guide on how to do it and make the best choice for you!

**Start by determining what you want** – the first step toward creating a bright future for yourself is being honest. Think about establishing your preferences and goals. You can go as specific as you like! Write down everything – from working hours to whether you would relocate for a career (at a certain point in life).

Prioritize the elements you feel the strongest about. Some of them are certainly more mandatory than others. These are your starting points.

**Do you have any skills?** – continue with listing all the skills you deem essential to your professional life. If the list is smaller than you expect, don't be discouraged! You are young, and time is on your side. Work toward developing some new skills you find interesting. After a while, you will be amazed by how long your skill list will get.

**Your potential career options** – write down the potential career options you have thought about. Yes, you can add more than one! Allow yourself to browse through the vastness of options – I encourage it! Having a few options will not only give you a sense of stability but it will also help you to open up your mind to something that you haven't even thought about before.

**Career requirements** – when it comes to expectations, it is a two-way street. Just as you expect something from a certain field or organization, they will expect something back from you. Are you ready to meet the expectations? Sit down and do your online research. Learn as much as possible about the career prospects, including experience and educational requirements. Learn about the most common responsibilities in the workplace.

**A fresh point of view** – following a certain profession or industry requires taking a peek into the future too. From all the ones you have lined up, which one seems like the best option for the future? As a young adult, you should consider this too. Society progresses, and as it does, it opens up new doors to the future, and at the same time it closes the ones to the past. Make an informed decision on the right option for you – one that will blast you into the world of tomorrow!

**Talk to a few experienced people** – you can start with the ones closest to you. If you have any relatives, or if your parents are involved in a field that you have taken an interest in, pick their brains a little bit. Remember that your research can be as extensive as you want, but it is a good idea to get some insight directly from the field too. A job can sound complicated on paper but simple in real life, and vice versa.

Do you have the option to visit their workspace? Jump with both feet to such an occasion!

**Start outlining your professional life** – it is all about managing your expectations while getting what you want! Outlining your professional path can help you create a solid strategy that will last you for years to come. It can give you the freedom to revise it whenever it is needed, possibly every one, two, or maybe even five years – it is all up to you. Project your needs onto the paper and see what it comes up with!

While I am on the subject, there is another thing you can do.

## Emerging Careers and Future Job Trends

I only touched upon the subject above, but I believe it piqued your interest. So far, we have determined that you might have one or several careers lined up – depending on your skills and requirements. As choosing a career is one of the most important aspects of life, young people are more and more keen on taking their time before deciding what they want (instead of jumping the gun and regretting it later on).

Yet again, we return to the question, "What do you enjoy doing?" to help you get to the desired destination. The wide range of options spans from one side to the other and keeping the future in mind is a good idea. As with every other teenager, you probably want to do a good job and enjoy doing it for a long time.

This leads me to the next section – start exploring some future job trends.

At this moment, you have little to no experience and limited knowledge of what makes the world go round. All that can change in an instant. Right now, everyone (not only young people) is in an uncertain environment where things can change just like that. Navigating through the challenge of searching for the perfect professional path in a constantly evolving society is a challenge – but not an impossible one!

There is always one good place to start, and that is beyond the voice of reason! I'm not saying that you should look for something completely unreasonable, but rather expand your horizons just a little beyond the reasonable choices you have made until now.

A factor of certainty is what you should include while doing this. Add that to your skillset, and you might end up uncovering a whole new world of emerging careers.

Just to get you started, here are a few of the most promising innovative job prospects of tomorrow.

**Software developers/computer managers** – the tech era as we know it is in full swing, and just at the right time! Gen Z is all about technology, paving the way for new emerging careers that will shape the world of tomorrow. For this particular one, you will become a valuable asset on the market. From writing codes to analyzing and maintaining platforms, there is nothing that you can't do with this job!

To give you an estimate, currently, the job market is open for people who have a bachelor's degree, and +5 years of experience.

Coursera has listed this as one of the most promising future jobs.

**Web developer** – another programming heaven for all you computer lovers! Nowadays, any brand or company needs to have its own website – and as a web developer, you can make that come true. Front-end, back-end, webmaster, and full-stack developer – these are the four main options to choose from. If programming languages are your biggest interest, then this might be the perfect option for you.

To give you an estimate, at the moment, the job market is only looking for people who have a degree, no experience is needed.

It requires a simple skillset, and since first created in the 1980s, the nature of this field has changed a few times. First, with the creation and vast use of the Internet, and then with the usage of mobile phones.

**Financial manager** – if numbers seem like the better choice, then achieving financial stability for a company must be a part of your dream, right? Profits and expenditures, strategizing about all the bigger decisions, and utilizing your planning and organizing skills to the fullest are what a financial manager is all about.

Are you looking into this? Companies are hiring – you need a bachelor's degree and +5 years of experience.

It is estimated that this particular job will achieve growth of about 17% in the next five years.

**Medical assistant** – providing support in hospitals is the dream of many young people. Do you consider yourself to be one of them? If a part of your skillset includes communicating with clients, if you have always been keen on pharmacy, and if you love helping doctors, then becoming a medical assistant is the perfect choice for you.

To become a medical assistant, you need professional training and a high school diploma. This is always a growing branch, with an estimated job growth of 18% in the next few years.

**Teacher** – since almost every aspect of today is moved online, why not this too? The future of teaching is online. Have you noticed you have the potential to lead a class rather than be a part of it? Spreading knowledge can be a wonderful thing and preparing the new generations to come for the world sounds like an excellent idea. So, why not add the online teacher option to your list too? Consider this a great way to utilize your abilities and grow your own business from scratch. There is a wide market for anything you are looking to offer. As it is increasing with every passing minute, you could share your knowledge with people from all over the world!

Did you know that there are more than 51 million YouTube Channels, and an average visitor spends about 40 minutes a day on this platform? That has to give you some boost to try creating something useful and uploading it there!

**Personal trainer** – more and more people are becoming aware of their body image, mostly due to social media. As a teenager, you must have witnessed that in your surroundings too. What you are probably not familiar with is because of the fast-paced life of today, not many people can keep up with their physical activities. This is where you come in. If your people skills are honed to perfection, if you love being active, and nurture a fondness toward the human body, have you thought about being a personal trainer?

A few things you should know here – you need certification, but not a degree, to become a personal trainer. You can choose to work inside or outside the gym. You need to nurture effective communication and an encouraging attitude. As a relatively new field, you can get as creative as you want. And finally, personal trainers are not dietitians or nutritionists.

These are some of the highest trending jobs that you can consider working toward. However unconventional it may sound, one of these might be the perfect fit for you.

When it comes to discovering more options for your future, I recommend first exploring your high school resources and what programs they offer. Plus, you can reach out to a school counselor and gather opinions.

No matter where you are in the world, I would recommend searching through various career groups on social networks, like Facebook, and connecting with other young individuals – both locally and globally. Or you don't even have to connect, just gather information and analyze the latest career trends. Not only do they share many tips and websites that can be of great help, but some may inspire you to discover your own path.

When it comes to leading global websites that can help you shape your journey and be inspired career-wise, LinkedIn should be on top of your list. Other useful sites are Indeed (one of the most popular job search engines worldwide and it is easily accessible to 53 countries), Monster (with a comprehensive database of career advice and tips), and CareerBuilder, etc.

In addition, career magazines like Harvard Business Review (HBR), Forbes, and Entrepreneur can prove to be valuable assets in your quest.

Simply Google any of these, and you will easily find them.

## Considering Non-Traditional and Unconventional Career Paths

Speaking of unconventional, I can notice the slight crest around your smile once this word is mentioned. So, if you are leaning more toward the creative side, there is a solution for you too! The job market is constantly changing, and the demand for certain skills changes too.

With a non-traditional career path, you might not get the linear progression you hope for, but you are in for a treat either way. As a young mind, it may even be the more logical way to shape your brain and delve deep into the professional world by choosing an unconventional path. Many industries allow for this due to the diverse skills that you can get from it.

Here are a few reasons why you should consider this:

✧ The right approach can help you land unique and adventurous job opportunities.

✧ Exploring many options can help you create a career that fits your lifestyle like a glove.

✧ You get to enjoy the freedom and flexibility that many people can't.

✧ The satisfaction of building something from 0 is immense.

✧ Presenting some new options results in passions that may be worth taking a second look at.

Again, I remind you of the question, "What do I want to do?" Think about what may benefit your future that still aligns with your goals and interests. Write down your passions and think about how to incorporate them into creating a new career path for yourself.

But how do you start looking for the right opportunities? Since people overall are on the rise looking for alternative ways of making money, why not join the club? As a teenager with a fresh perspective, you have plenty to offer. Here are a few ways how you can use your skills and start building your career:

✧ Think about having a "side hustle." This is for those who want to take on some freelance tasks. It is a great way to start learning the tips and tricks of successful freelancers. Also, it is a great way to see how your skills have progressed and how proficient you are at finishing certain tasks.

✧ Look into start-up businesses. They are the perfect way to start your business venture with a little help. Create a solid business plan that is unique and shows a fresh perspective, and then start researching ways to complete it!

✧ Online ventures are on the list too. So far, digital ventures are considered a phenomenon in the global economy. If you have an idea you need to bring into existence, then take a leap of faith! It just might be worth it.

Remember, exploring career options does not have to be a hassle or a task. Make it as enjoyable as you can. I hope that you will consider these notes and start working toward your goal. Consider this a rewarding experience, where every step is equally important. Open yourself up to a whole new world of possibilities – but not before you've reached the end of this book!

That said, in the next chapter, we will go into detail on how to develop essential skills.

CHAPTER 3

# DEVELOPING ESSENTIAL SKILLS

> *"Tell me, and I forget, teach me and I may remember, involve me and I learn."*
>
> — *Benjamin Franklin*

Welcome to the chapter where I help you develop some essential skills needed to succeed in the workplace. Now, these essential skills are not necessarily all the ones that you have already written down. For example, marketing, management, technical, or computer skills are all good, but you can't really use them if you don't have (or work on) your soft skills.

The difference is that, unlike hard skills, you display soft skills in each situation where you converse with another person.

These are different from the ones you can learn in school. Most of them are typically learned through life experiences and the people you see as role models. Interestingly, as you grow, before you plunge yourself into the job market, you never notice that you are learning them as you go.

The subconscious part of the entire learning process is quite interesting. You do that by mimicking the behavior of a person you admire, by rationally trying to judge a situation based on facts instead of emotions, and of course, my favorite – learning from your mistakes.

All of this means that you are growing. So, when the time comes to determine which skills you excel at and which ones need honing, this is where you become fully aware of yourself as an individual. There is a highlighted importance to these skills that can make you stand out from a crowd (if utilized properly).

Now, I am encouraging you to look upon your past experiences, every situation that has taught you something. If this confuses you, allow me to help you. Let's take a look at how to identify your soft skills.

## Identifying and Enhancing Your Transferable Skills

First things first – what are transferable skills? These are the soft skills you can transfer from one job position to another. Most of them are not technical by nature, and they all help you get the job done.

They are also known as soft skills – a group of important abilities that enhance your competence in the professional field. Every employer is interested in them. Even if you want to make it out on your own, you still need them to make yourself more available, presentable, and more successful at what you want to do.

Now, determining your transferable skills requires some introspection. Answer yourself this – is there anything you are naturally better at than the people around you? As you grow, have you noticed that you are better at certain things? Each time you have worked in a group, was there a task that was consistently (and I mean always) done by none other than you?

*That is your strong side.*

All you need to do is start building upon that. Grab a pen and paper and start writing down every skill that you have noticed about yourself. It can be anything from a good trait (such as good communication with others) to your high levels of empathy and resilience!

Identifying these non-academic skills can help you figure out how well you can adapt to various conditions – in your professional and personal life too. Consider them the tools you need to thrive in a cultural, social, and professional setting.

At some point, while writing these down, you may start wondering what good these skills will do for you. Are these skills really that important that you should focus on them so much? Or should you just look the other way and ignore them? I'm here to nudge you in the right direction and to tell you to stick this one out! There are many reasons why this is important. Any professional setting values them because:

- ✧ By having them, you enjoy support and success in any workplace.
- ✧ You can stand out with them in an interview with an employer.
- ✧ Add them to your CV to make it worth taking a second look at.
- ✧ Whenever you apply for a promotion, having soft skills is perfect for accentuating (how it helped you navigate your position and relationships with others).
- ✧ Even if you want to make it on your own, they are much needed, especially since, all jobs include some form of communication with clients.

The best thing about transferable skills is that they are called that because you can use them at any job! That makes it essential for you to recognize and accentuate them even more!

You have probably managed to create a list of skills by now. Now, let's further break down this exercise into two bits.

**The first step** is to write down the competence level (it can be a number from 1-10 or 1-5, whatever suits you best) next to each of them. It is important to be realistic about yourself so you can get the best results out of this exercise. Some competencies might get a 10; some might get a six or even a two – and that's okay! Look at the numbers and note the ones with a lower number. That gives you an idea of what you need to focus on. Whether it is a time management skill, or the power to work well in a team, if it needs your attention, do everything it takes to improve it.

There are many ways to enhance transferable skills – some of those ways include:

- ✧ Taking one or even a few online courses or maybe watching YouTube channels that provide such presentations.

- ✧ Volunteering someplace that will get you a step closer to working with people in order to develop your 'people skills.'

- ✧ Put yourself in a teaching position and share your knowledge and wisdom with others.

These are just a few to begin with, but the truth is, once you start looking, you will see that there is a whole world of options that provide you with a way to hone your soft skills.

**The next step** is to take a good look at your list and find out what is missing. Yes, this is something you might not have thought of until this moment. But there are so many soft skills that you are bound to forget about a few of them. Does your list need to include some literacy skills? Maybe organizational skills? Or some stress management skills? Yes, there is a lot where that came from too!

Do your research and add all the ones you find on the Internet. They can help you widen your horizons and paint a new picture of what you can perfect and achieve within this section.

On that note, I have separated some of the most important ones for you – how to build and make the most out of them so they can help you thrive in a professional environment! Take a look!

## Communication, Teamwork, Problem-Solving, and Critical Thinking Skills

According to the World Economic Forum report on the future of jobs, these are some of the most wanted transferable skills! Increase your value by working on enriching them with every passing moment. Here is a straightforward way on how you can do that for each one.

### *Communication*

How you provide information to the people you work with and the clients you work for is a vital aspect of any job. Considering how they wish to receive the information you provide is one of the ways you can be proficient at this soft skill in particular. As a teenager, do you think you have what it takes to master the art of communication?

Sharing and giving information – communicating – is a vital part of life not just in a professional setting either. It is everywhere around us, and it comes in many forms. You have already encountered them – a verbal, a non-verbal, a written, or even a visual form.

The most important bit here is knowing how to give and receive clear and concise information.

As a teenager who has grown up amid the Internet and technology boom, you may know much more about communication than you think. Adults a few decades back used the telephone as a means of communication. Then along came emails, texting, and social media. Nowadays, communication is made easier in theory, but not everyone can do it.

What happened?

Ease of access meant losing the proper dialogue needed to establish a relationship with whoever was on the "other end of the line." In effect, newer generations (including you) lost the ability to communicate effectively. Communication's most essential aspects include patience, listening, understanding, and controlling your thoughts and emotions in order to get the best outcome for your situation. Because of today's culture, like many young people, you may have been neglecting this skill most of your life, it is only natural not to know how to properly establish a relationship in any setting, not just a professional one.

Thankfully, that can be fixed!

It all starts with the simplest thing – eye contact. Whenever you have the opportunity to talk to someone, there are many things you can do to make yourself more presentable and to successfully open up the lines of communication. Here are some other ways you can practice in order to improve your communication skills:

- ✧ Start paying attention when someone is talking to you. Make a scheme in your mind and pinpoint the essential things so you can reciprocate.

- ✧ Work on using clear language. You don't have to make your sentences long and complex – sometimes, the simplest answer is the most effective.

- ✧ Use body language to your advantage. Sometimes non-verbal communication says more than words do. Practice standing up straight, using a calm tone of voice, appropriate gestures, and gentle facial expressions.

- ✧ Ask for feedback whenever you can. This is an exercise best done within a circle of people you are comfortable with. Ask your parents, relatives, or teacher if they find your communication skills to be improving.

- ✧ Speak up when something is not clear. Start from the smallest thing – when you see that something is not very clear to you, asking questions about it is a great way to clear the air of any assumptions.

- ✧ Work on your confidence. Last but not least, consider your level of confidence as a driving force that pushes you forward into the professional world. Invest a small portion of your day to work on it, and soon, you will see some incredible changes.

Communication is great, but once you've mastered communicating with a single person, can you manage to do the same with more people at the same time?

## *Teamwork*

The meaning of Teamwork is communication and navigating several relationships at the same time. It improves equality and the ability to recognize the strengths and weaknesses of each person in the group. An additional benefit is that it provides excellent opportunities to work with various types of people.

Do you consider yourself to be a team player? Do you know that being a good team player is one of the key aspects of success? Taking pride in being able to adapt to change is a good thing, so make sure to accentuate it whenever possible.

But what happens to those that don't have the high level of skills for this?

As a teenager, you might find yourself in a difficult position if you are unable to be a team player. Some of us are followers, others are leaders, but everyone can fit the model of being a team player. If you have written this down on your paper and put a low grade next to it, then it is time to take some action!

Here are some tips to get you started!

Generally, it is a bit difficult to teach a person how to become a team player from scratch, but thankfully, there are a few exercises that can help you hone this skill to perfection. Other than communication being a pillar of a good team, here are a few other things to consider exploring:

✧ Define the relationship by making clear everyone's role in the group. Any group at the beginning may seem like total chaos, but that is only until responsibilities are divided up. Once that happens, everyone understands their duties and tasks, avoiding confusion and repetition, and thus creating a seamless experience.

✧ Focus on collaborating too. If you don't know how to become an equal participant in a group, then have a discussion. Talking about it can clear the air and give you the floor whenever you want to share an idea or a thought. Also, this way, the entire group promotes compromise and encourages everyone to contribute with their valuable and unique perspectives.

✧ There is no group without trust. Practicing trust starts from something small and develops over time into the biggest support the group will have. If you haven't worked in a team until now, you might not have experienced this, but after working in one for a while, you will start to feel a certain level of integrity that the group exhibits. It becomes a supportive and reliable space where everyone is equal in terms of sharing concerns and ideas.

✧ The team shares the strike or the win together! It doesn't matter if it is a win or a loss; a team always sticks together. When the collective objectives are met because you know that you have worked hard enough as a team to reach the goal, then you also have the grounds for the celebration together as well.

✧ Learn as much as you can. At the end of the day, the team is comprised of many different people. All of them, along with their unique points of view, traits, and responsibilities, can give you a free platform to learn! It is the perfect opportunity for personal and professional growth, so whenever you have the chance, jump at the idea of being a part of a team!

As you can see, being in a team is a continuous process and you can't learn much after only one day. However, spending some time being a part of one may end up with you acquiring many fruitful results.

Every team has its ups and downs. What happens when you reach a low point and need to resolve a certain issue?

## Problem-Solving

There is so much happening in the world right now that it is impossible to avoid stress. Unpleasant situations can stand there, waiting around every corner. As a teenager, you might have encountered a lot of them, or you may have only experienced a small amount. Either way, you must learn they are an inevitable part of our day-to-day life.

In the professional setting, a failure or a mistake can bring on a large amount of stress. I have seen this happen many times on various occasions. Sometimes, the situation escalated to become even bigger than it was, and in other cases, it was resolved almost immediately. Do you know what contributes to this outcome?

Having problem-solving skills. The ability to analyze a certain situation (and de-escalate it if needed) is a much-needed skill in every professional environment. Any teenager would be lucky to master this skill, as it is imperative for success in an individual and group setting as well. Developing and presenting problem-solving skills can help you to thrive.

For those that feel stuck...

If your problem-solving skills are not up to par, remember you can always do something about it. Nowadays, plenty of exercises and tips will get you started working on it. Here, practicality is key, so try to push yourself whenever you are in a tricky situation. The following are some practical tips for you below:

- ✧ Try to calm your mind down. If you are a person that doesn't work well under stress, do some stress relieving exercises. It can be anything from slowly breathing in and out for a few seconds, counting back from 20, or anything else that works for you. The purpose is to create a calm and collected environment within.

- ✧ Collect all the facts. If you don't know where to begin, simply follow the trail of information. Whenever you are faced with an issue, start by gathering information about it. What happened, how many people are involved, what's at stake? Look at it as if you were solving a puzzle – you need to tie all the pieces together. Once you do that, the solution usually stares you right in the face.

✧ Always look for a pattern. If you are wise enough, you will start looking for patterns at an early age. The mind of the average teenager might not go that far, but I am here to help you overcome that challenge. Each time you evaluate a tricky situation, try to look for a pattern of behavior. Start with yourself and expand your circle as you go, including your peers along the way. Try to find a connection to why something is happening (especially if it occurs repeatedly).

✧ Think outside the box. Yes, you have heard this many times before, but for a good reason. Coming up with alternative and creative solutions for challenges and issues can help you develop in unimaginable ways. Don't try to limit yourself to conventional approaches. Take up the exercise of creating a fictitious problem. Then, think of at least three ways to solve it. It is called training your mind.

✧ After you have come up with a valuable solution – enforce it! The sooner you take action to mend an issue – the better the results will be. This is slightly connected to the previous point. Sometimes, the first solution will backfire. And that's okay. It is why you have a few tricks up your sleeve – use them wisely!

✧ Don't give up. The most important thing to remember is not to give up on this. Take this as a personal note rather than a tip. Building up soft skills such as this takes time, so practice persistence. Learn how to make yourself think better with every challenge you face until your skill becomes next to perfection.

As we move on from the subject of problem-solving skills, I couldn't help but look forward to the last bit. Completing the circle with the last skill – critical thinking.

## Critical Thinking

Instilling all of these key skills that scream leadership position means focusing deeply on each of them. The final one includes the art of critical thinking. Have you always found yourself to be a fairly reasonable person that is open-minded, a little bit skeptical, but always with respect toward precision and different points of view? Then, you are a valuable critical thinker.

These individuals tend to analyze any situation, observe, and evaluate it based on their information. The language of Michael Scriven and Richard Paul (2003) defines critical thinking as:

> *"Critical thinking is the intellectually disciplined process of actively and skillfully conceptualizing, applying, analyzing, synthesizing, and/or evaluating information gathered from, or*

*generated by observation, experience, reflection, reasoning, or communication, as a guide to belief and action."*

What happens if you feel like you don't have it?

There is a certain discipline to learning everything – apply that in this situation as well. As a teenager, learn how to use critical thinking to your advantage. It is the last piece of the puzzle from this section that can shape you into a phenomenal professional.

Enhancing your critical thinking skills can be done with the assistance of the following tips:

✧ Evaluation should be the first thing on your mind. Evaluate everything from your sources, to how you filter the information into a relevant and irrelevant pile, and also, whether you challenge any assumptions or leave them hanging in the air. This is the first aspect of critical thinking. Developing a heightened sense of reasoning is key.

✧ Listen to the arguments and sources. As a critical thinker, you need to consider all the arguments you encounter during challenging situations, as well as the sources of those arguments. Again, an excellent exercise is to come up with a fictional issue. Develop the issue like it is a scene from a crime book. Come up with a few peers with various backgrounds and expertise and then think about their claims. Go step by step and explain your thought process to yourself.

Consider multiple perspectives, however "out there" they may be. Creating such a scenario can help you develop a certain "voice of reason," where you only conclude based on facts.

✧ Ask the right questions. Have you ever noticed how the most difficult question to answer is… "Why?" Do you know that is the only way to fully explore an issue? You stimulate your practice-thinking abilities this way and you may be surprised by all the answers you get.

✧ Always, and I mean always, broaden your horizons. This is not something you can only apply in this case but in every other aspect of life too. Reading books, articles, and research papers can help you broaden your knowledge on any subject and help you feel like you are doing something to improve your critical thinking skills.

While I am on the subject of books, read as much as you can! For example, finishing this one will give you plenty of insight into what you want to do, be, and achieve in life. So, keep going!

## Developing Digital Literacy and Technological Proficiency

After we have taken a good look at the most important skills together, it is time to go through another section that includes transferable skills from the 21st century. So far, I have delved into the subject of skills that have been around for a long period of time. But at this point, after you have mastered the ones above, it is time to look toward the future.

Being proficient in technology is a must for anyone these days. Whether you are a teenager, an adult, or even a senior, you are bound to adapt to the lifestyle of the world we live in now. It involves plenty of technology everywhere you turn. So, how does this apply to a professional environment?

Imagine having your own company and looking to employ a handful of people. The company can be in any sector, starting from IT and finishing up in the fashion field. As you go through the interview process, you come across an applicant with no digital literacy (almost impossible in this day and age but humor me for the sake of argument). Would you consider employing them if you knew how much time it would take to educate them on the subject of technological proficiency? Yes, it does seem like an unnecessary challenge, right?

Being skilled in digital literacy means knowing how to look for and filter relevant information precisely, quickly, and safely. This is more than just knowing how to use a computer. It is the act of browsing safely and being professional while doing it. It is a skill that will help you become a lifelong learner.

If you put your mind to it a little bit, you will realize that digital technologies are ever-changing. Nothing is constant. Even though this results in an array of flexible ways that help you to learn and work, you need to know how to keep up with the latest trends.

Being digitally literate can help you integrate into any field you want. Do you want to know what it takes to make that happen? Be mindful of the following tips:

✧ You should start from scratch. Yes, as a young person raised in the digital era, I know this sounds kind of weird, but hear me out. You need to familiarize yourself with the simplest of tasks, such as file management, knowing your way around all operating systems, creating spreadsheets, and knowing how to present the information. Many features might have slipped through your fingers, so take a few steps back and explore.

✧ Learn how to stay safe on the Internet. As beautiful a place as it can be, it is also the place of predators, information thieves, and more. Knowing how to be cautious when sharing information on the web is a part of being proficient in digital language.

✧ Even if you are not into coding, programming, or software development, you still need to stay on track with the latest developments in the field. That way, you can present another way of staying on top of a situation. Participating in a few courses or online forums can help you continuously build your knowledge.

✧ Experiment for creative freedom. Let's face it, eventually, with any work you do, you will want a little bit of freedom for your creative side to shine through. Pick the digital world as the most useful tool to make that happen. Challenge yourself –

resolve issues using technology, learn through the trial-and-error process, and make the most out of it.

✧ Talk to people. However out of the blue this might seem, talking to peers that are as equally involved in the digital world as you may open up some fresh possibilities for you. Exchange ideas and discuss projects – it is how you can grow and deepen your knowledge.

Digital literacy will always evolve and grow. Being a teenager, it should not be difficult to adopt a growth mindset and be open to all the opportunities technology can provide you with!

## Cultivating Emotional Intelligence and Adaptability

Well, well, well – we have slowly reached the topic that most teenagers avoid – emotional intelligence. But, instead of boring you with details, I am here to tell you that you can express your emotional intelligence in a healthy manner that can also help you evolve in the working arena.

Do you know what emotional intelligence means? *It is the ability to define and take control of your emotions and recognize the feelings of those around you.*

On the other hand, *adaptability is the capacity to adjust to ever-changing conditions.*

Do you know how you can develop both of these transferable skills?

The simplest answer is to create a higher level of self-awareness. The emotions you deal with as a teenager may be overwhelming at times – it is a normal process, as you are still learning how to put them under control. By being a little gentler toward yourself, you can notice which things trigger you and how you react to them, thus getting to the core of you.

Another thing – the people around you (especially in a professional setting) count on you to think on your feet and with a cool head. But that doesn't mean you should quickly dismiss all your feelings and act like a robot. Find the balance where you can validate the feelings of others and show empathy but still act professionally.

Practice active listening skills but learn how to create a barrier where it does not personally affect you or change your opinion in any way. All of this can be a handful in the beginning, so I suggest you take things slow and one at a time.

Showing a healthy and appropriate approach will only result in maturity and success. Calmly dealing with any changes that may come your way is the best way to take full control of a situation and come out on the other side like a true winner!

Did all of this seem like too much for you to handle? After all, you are still very young, and you have yet to expand your knowledge and skills, but with clear guidance, you will tackle this seemingly complex subject. That leads us to the next chapter – finding the perfect guidance!

# CHAPTER 4

# SEEKING GUIDANCE

*"Wisdom is the best guide and faith is the best companion."*

*Dalai Lama*

**B**ut what happens in those times when you feel like you have lost any sense of direction? However hard you try, and however clear your goal may be, sometimes you might get the feeling of being stuck. You feel like all the research and theory that you have done is simply not good enough.

This is the time to start experiencing the practice bit, not only the theory bit. After all, by plunging yourself into the professional world you step into the unknown without a safety net. Deciding what you want to be when you grow up is a tough question.

Instead of putting yourself under a lot of pressure by trying to accomplish everything on your own, why not try to seek out some guidance? Take the pressure off and create a safe space for you to thrive. I am giving you some insight on how to pave the road to success with the help of others.

## The Role of Mentors and Role Models

Many studies have shown the importance of mentoring. All humans learn as much as possible by watching, then mimicking someone else's behavior. It has always been the easiest way to learn. Being a teenager, it is especially important to surround yourself with people you look up to, people who can positively influence your existence, and help you develop an understanding of the professional world.

Think about what kind of learning experience you want to gain. Also, try to answer this question – who do you look up to the most? Why? The role models and mentors should be people who are active participants in the community. They should be able to thrive in a professional and/or a personal setting, and they should also be able to offer you a plateau of educational and career aspirations.

There is a slight difference between a mentor and a role model. Here is a brief explanation of both.

**Mentor** – a mentor is a person who has plenty of experience in a specific professional field and possesses the skillset that you lack. As a teenager and a less experienced individual, they support your transitioning process from the safe environment of a classroom to the rollercoaster of the real world.

More often, they provide you with examples of how to think and act in the most common situations. I encourage every teenager to have a mentor – it can be anyone – a teacher from school, someone you admire, someone from your workplace. Ask them if they would assist you and take it from there!

**Role model** – the role model is not necessarily someone who can show you how to properly act, but rather show you the importance of differentiating between bad and good. A role model often presents positive and negative examples to help you understand both and to choose the right one.

Also, role models can be people you choose unconsciously. This starts from your early childhood, as you are drawn into the behavior of the people you see most often – your parents, relatives, teachers, etc. Who is your role model? Have you noticed something about them you liked so much, you started implementing it yourself?

Both are considered equally important since they can boost both morale and motivation. Their role in shaping your future includes the following:

✧ You get inspired. Whether it is a mentor or a role model, they are oftentimes more experienced than you are. Note their stories, their challenges, and the obstacles they had to overcome. Allow them to teach you how to navigate through your work with the help of the knowledge you have accumulated over the years.

✧ Take the advice. Despite how much stubbornness there may be within you, give them some space to help you. A career decision is a challenging process, so once you decide to seek assistance, let them help prepare you for a particular profession.

✧ Deepen your skillset. Having the proper set of skills is the jumping point that will help you stand out from the crowd tomorrow. Most of these skills include the transferable skills I talked about in the previous chapter. Mentors are especially important here, as they give you a better insight into skills such as communication, navigating through a professional environment, the power of a successful presentation, etc.

✧ Write down all the contacts. Both the mentor and the role model can be of invaluable worth when it comes to getting you in touch with the right people. They can help you create a beneficial network and make you more visible to the most important people and companies in the industry.

This is only the beginning – getting a taste of what you want sounds like a dream. But there is still a lot to cover, so let's move on to the next guidance step.

## Utilizing Resources Like Career Counseling and Guidance Services

You are a part of the generation that will be the driving force that moves the world forward. Having this in mind, utilizing all the available resources to be the positive change in the world takes bringing out "the big shot" resources like career counseling.

It is a beneficial step that will lead you in the right direction and to the desired career path. Getting in touch with a career counselor is the push you need. As an individual, you are in a transitioning period, because as soon as your teenage years are over, you will become a valuable asset in the job marketplace.

Career counseling and guidance are the steps you can take to identify career opportunities that you are otherwise unable to uncover by yourself. The first step to take is to talk to a teacher, your school counselor, or a career advisor and start gathering information.

All of them may provide you with various tidbits of information, so once you set up an appointment with them, get the most out of your one-on-one with them. In the previous chapter, you created a list of the strengths (your skills) and rated them. Take that list with you and discuss it with them. You won't believe how valuable their input will be.

If you want to get the proper guidance, then you also need to share all your accomplishments up until that point with them. Gather your information about your education, your grades, your hobbies, your interests, and every extra-curricular activity you have undertaken such as internships, etc. All this information can provide an insight into who you are, and can be extremely valuable to any counselor who is trying to help you.

They will give you a lot of tips and steps you can take. They will teach you how to explore job descriptions, and they will help you learn how to research multiple occupations. In the meantime, after reviewing every bit of the information you have provided them with, they will let you know if you need to obtain any additional qualifications for the field you have in mind. On top of all that, a career counselor will also guide you through any of the alternatives as well.

Last but not least, they will provide you with some online platforms to help you with your career exploration. They will help you to evaluate the potential for growth, and to teach you how to search for the best opportunities within the salary range.

## Networking and Informational Interviews

Have you heard of the term networking? If your core goal includes finding the perfect job field for you, then you probably have. But not all teenagers know what it means. Networking represents getting in touch with any of the connections you have obtained during your time researching the job market. The target of networking is to build a relationship with companies and individuals who can, in the present or the future, give you plenty of advice, information, or a professional opportunity.

An informal interview is a vessel through which you deepen your relationships with the contacts from your network. Consider them as an opportunity to expand and get some useful info from a simple conversation.

Before you begin, you need to know how important this step is. As a teenager, from the informal interview, you will gain:

✧ Information about how you actually do a specific job. You will get the real picture of what it is like to occupy a certain position, rather than learning from your idea about it.

✧ Insight about how it is to work in a real environment, with real issues, and real rewards. Sometimes, the stress can be almost overwhelming, at other times, you may enjoy every second of your time spent there.

✧ Knowledge about how to get to where you want to be. With a few strategic steps, you can get into the field of your choosing.

Now, you have opened the doors of communication and you have set up an interview. You have done everything –

from gathering information about the person you are meeting to collecting all the information about yourself. These are all proper steps but, once the interview begins, what are you going to ask whoever is on the other side?

Allow me to be of service. Below you will find a set of questions that you can consider as a starting point. Go over them, think about which answers you want to get, and how you can deepen the conversation on each question. Consider these questions as a way to take control of the interview and to get all the information you need. Here they are:

- ✧ Ask the other party to describe a day in their life. What types of situations do they encounter, and how do they deal with them?

- ✧ What are their interests? Is there something they like a lot, and something they strongly dislike? It can be anything from getting up early in the morning, to a special routine.

- ✧ The steps they took to get to where they are right now. Opportunities, formal education, expanding their skillset – everything it took!

- ✧ How many mistakes did they make along the way? Did that greatly impact their current position? Would they change something from their past?

- ✧ Why choose the field they are in at the moment? Are they planning on sticking with it for a long time, and what surprises came with the job?

✧ Ask them to give a piece of advice to a youngster like yourself.

✧ Can they recommend someone else for you to talk to? It is a great way to further expand your network.

Networking and getting information from informal interviews are great ways to get ahead on your quest for a successful professional life. Here is another extra step you can take to make that happen.

## Engaging With Online Communities and Professional Organizations

There is another way to gain all the relevant data about job prospects – seeking guidance from professional organizations and online communities. Over the past few decades, these two options have become pillars of the thriving community we live in today. There are many, many options out there, all you need to do is begin your research.

✧ Identify the communities that can help you. It is important to locate the ones you share the same interests and goals with – it is how you will get the most out of the experience.

✧ Being online is easier – you are only a few clicks away from finding a community that aligns with your career goals. Once you find it, become an active member of it. Ask questions and take part in discussions. Soon you will realize you have expanded your network beyond your wildest imagination.

✧ Engage as much as you can. Virtual events, webinars, volunteering, taking up an internship, and sharing your journey with others – establish yourself as a knowledgeable member of the community and open up a path for further engagements and networking opportunities.

Sometimes, when you are too close to a certain situation, you might get caught up in it and set some unrealistic expectations. Guidance from a third party is the best way to tackle the situation. It is your responsibility to set up a support and guidance system for yourself. That way, you can help yourself move further along the path of creating a bright professional future for yourself.

With this, you get some help for the next step, which is planning for education and training. Let's go through the subject together.

## CHAPTER 5

# PLANNING FOR EDUCATION AND TRAINING

> "Education is the passport for the future, for tomorrow belongs to those who prepare for it today."
>
> — *Malcolm X*

P lanning for your future sounds like one of the most exciting things to do. Considering this will be one of your biggest life changes, it is only fair to do it your way. At least mostly, right? However, that still doesn't change the fact that you are a teenager and might not know what you want or how to get it. But don't let this discourage you.

There will be moments when you feel doubtful about your choices. Then it is best to simply take a deep breath and try to remind yourself that you don't need to rush. Put one foot in front of the other at a pace that suits you – after all, these are major life choices, and it is best to be handled with great care and research on your part.

Concentrating on educational and vocational plans may help you identify yourself better and help you reach financial stability. When you focus on all your lists, wishes and plans, and get support from the people around you, you know you are headed in the right direction.

As a starting point, review your options. Do they require special education or simpler training? This act of evaluating the steps needed to get to a certain position is called career planning. As a teenager, you think you have all the time in the world. Be careful here, you should avoid shifting to a slower gear and letting go of your professional dreams.

Instead, it is time to delve deeper into your options. Let's go!

## Exploring Post-Secondary Education Options

It is vital to understand that whichever option you choose, you should probably not do it at the last minute. Yes, choosing a career path is a challenge in and of itself, but that does not mean you need to procrastinate until the last minute. Remember, you are getting into a pretty competitive world out there, so start your engine now!

Make sure to have collected all the necessary documents and submit them before the deadline. Check the admission periods for all the schools you are interested in and underline them as important dates!

This is the importance of sticking to a plan. Do you know the answer to the question "What do I want to do after school?" – If not, then make a note of it to answer it before your final year of school begins. During that summer, you can give yourself time to think and research all the options – are you going to college, do you want to undergo vocational training, join the military, or get a job?

It helps to talk with a person that you consider close. This can be your friend, maybe a family member, or even a professional. During this period, it is important to keep focusing on improving your skills, both technical and soft.

Once you become ready to start preparing yourself for the next chapter of your life, it is time to dive deep and take some action! Once school's out, you can start doing plenty of things to prepare yourself for the next chapter. Here are a handful of things that should absolutely be a part of your list:

- ✧ Start visiting trade schools and colleges. Consider it the most important step you need to take, and that is why you are doing it earlier than expected. Planning your future means deep research, so why not start visiting universities beforehand? Explore the different campuses and see what types of degree programs they offer. It will become an invaluable experience. You can differentiate between what they offer in theory and how they achieve it in practice.

✧ Start job-shadowing someone. It kind of sounds like a mentor, but it's a whole other thing. Once you have decided on a particular branch you'd like to get involved in, it is important to shatter the glass ideal of what the job is supposed to look like. Rather than creating your idea of what the responsibilities and workflow will look like, take a more "hands-on" approach. Shadowing a person who works in the field of your interest is a great way to get the feel of it without actually working.

✧ Start volunteering. Extra-curricular activities are just as important as academic achievements when applying to a university (or anywhere else). Also, getting some valuable experience can only enhance you as an applicant and person ready to dive into the professional world. Inquire about some volunteering spots in your town. There is a high chance you'll find one that fits right with your interests and skill set. Help others and help yourself through the process as well.

✧ Take note of what you need to improve. A skill set is something that you can focus on and improve at all times. If you need to boost your creative thinking process – focus on that. If you need to improve your presentation skills – focus on that, and so on. I believe you get the picture on this one, so get to work!

✧ Brainstorm the next year. The last year of your studies will go by in a flash. Thankfully, it is time to start looking into some activities and skills you haven't tried so far. Be mindful that some of them can help you get some leadership skills, and skills to become an excellent teammate. Read about the available courses and choose one (or a few) that seem like a good fit.

## Evaluating the Importance of Higher Education for Specific Career Paths

Sometimes, it takes a little bit of time to realize what you want to do in life. And that is fine. There is an undeniable stability in wanting to take the year off and explore your options a little further. Of course, it only works if you truly commit to it.

However, before you immediately jump to the conclusion that maybe taking a year off or focusing on working for a while before you get to your dream might set you back a bit. Why? In most cases, there is a certain importance in higher education, especially if your career path leads you right to it.

For many teenagers, having a higher education means getting into a specific field of work and achieving success. While there are many professions out there that require no university degree, many of them still do.

Think about this for a while - even if your preferred career choice does not require you to continue your formal education, if you have the chance to go to university, why not take it?

Are you looking for a way to enhance your learning skills? Higher education can make you more prepared, help shape you as a person and provide you with the option of career maturity, adaptability, and a sense of belonging.

Allow me to elaborate further. Some careers require a traditional approach, and here are a few to begin with:

**If you are going into medicine.** Do you think becoming a healthcare professional without any higher education is possible? If this is one of your choices, then you absolutely need to comb through all the universities that provide graduate programs that will get you a step closer to achieving your goal. Whether it is a nursing program or medical school, you need to be adequately prepared, especially in those cases where another life is at stake.

**If you are going for a legal profession.** Are you dreaming about becoming a lawyer or a judge? Your dream will only nudge you in the right direction. It requires plenty of work and studying hard. Also, it cannot be achieved without formal training. Every legal professional undergoes a graduate and even a post-graduate program. Through these programs, you get the ability to understand and learn complex legal concepts. You will also enjoy the perk of building your network while in law school.

**If you are going into education.** There is no way you become a part of the educational system without the proper education, because it will be you that one day shapes the minds of the future. Obtaining a degree in teaching will open up a realm of possibilities for you. It can help you make the transition from a teenager yourself to someone who helps teenagers in the future become who they want to be.

**If you are going into science.** There are more than a few reasons why going into the field of science requires investing in higher education. You will not only enjoy the perks of the wider network, but also you will gain expertise, guidance, and research opportunities, as well as laboratories so advanced that you'll get to learn some pretty spectacular things! On top of that, gaining better data analysis skills and using scientific methodology while obtaining your scientific research degree will make you feel even more fulfilled!

**If you are going into engineering.** Due to the fast advancements in technology, it is no wonder why so many young people want to be a part of this ever-growing world. Being one of them yourself is a great idea! If you have always had a knack for building and creating things and have shown a special kind of admiration toward technology, then this is the field for you. But don't be fooled into thinking that a few YouTube crash courses are the equivalent of higher education. Obtain a degree in computer science, information technology, or engineering. It is a field requiring a certain level of specialization to thrive.

These are just a handful of options that require a formal higher education. But if these are not on your list, there is no need to feel discouraged! In the next section, we go through some alternatives that you might find incredibly useful!

## Considering Alternatives to Traditional Education

We live in a world where looking for alternatives to college has become increasingly popular, and it is getting more socially acceptable by the minute. Teenagers fail to realize that this practice has existed since the dawn of time. Every generation has that "revelation moment" where they realize there are many alternatives to be considered.

For some teenagers, college is still an essential and wonderful experience. But, for those who wish to take a more alternative path toward creating a bright future, many options are right here waiting for you! Does your teenage intuition tell you that maybe college is not the right choice for you? Before making a long-term commitment that you might regret, pause. Let me help you think outside the box for a bit.

Your career goal should be your main focus, and getting there is only a part of the process. So, look into some of the options that I have laid out for you and see if one of them appeals to your senses:

**An apprenticeship** – the delicate art of training for a career as a carpenter, an electrician, and so much more lies in the form of an apprenticeship. This is an incredible way to get the most out of your training and enter the workforce as a worker with plenty of skills! After an apprenticeship, you can easily get licensed (granted after you are under strict surveillance and training for a specified time period). Take this as an alternative to traditional education but know that it too takes a while to complete it.

**Community college** – you might have only heard about this option until now but don't know what it is. So far, this has been the most popular alternative to university studies, mostly because of the accessibility point of view. A community college is a fantastic option that offers various programs – one of which will surely be up to your liking. This is an excellent chance if you are considering attending a school close to your home. The perfect option if you want to take on a job while working. Do you wish to get the feel of a higher education without going through the entire four-year challenge? Community college is the answer.

**Online learning** – the vastness of the Internet shows no limits! All you need to do is find the right course that fits your needs. Dedicate a few hours of your day to learning what you love. After some time, you will find yourself filled with knowledge and skills that you could have only dreamt about obtaining in such a short time! What I love the most about the Internet is that anyone can use it as an educational tool. Why not do that yourself? View it as a means to improve overall performance and expertise. Take some free courses or pay for a few courses if necessary! Either way, as long as you are determined and pass the classes with flying colors, you will have a list of employers or clients waiting for you.

**A vocational education** – one of the fastest-growing college alternatives is the trade schools. It seems that although they cost a little less than a more formal higher education, they are still the preferred choice of many. Any teenager wanting a streamlined path toward becoming a part of the workforce should try this. Why waste your time sitting in classes you have no interest in? Instead, spend your time wisely – learning what you are interested in!

**An employment** – you might be one of those individuals that want to get right into building their portfolio with employment – right out of high school. In today's world, getting a job after finishing your secondary education and working your way up the ladder to a position you choose is more possible than ever. Even though, as a worker, you will encounter many challenges along the way (and during the application process, too), it might be worth your while. Many employers nowadays value the possibility of career advancement through both employment and education, so if you are up for a challenge like this one, I encourage you to take the next step.

**Social media** – as you can see, in today's world, there are many more options than you can think of. One of those options includes having a full-time career as a content creator or a social media personality. This is an option that was not available 10 or 15 years ago. Even though it is a relatively new field, it attracts more and more people every day. If this is your dream job, then you might want to learn something more about it. Many young people start with this, but only a few succeed. The key is having an entrepreneurial and dedicated spirit, so good luck!

**Entrepreneurship** – instead of getting a degree or a 9-5 job, you can always focus on building something from the ground up yourself! Turn that dream into reality with the help of some meticulous entrepreneurship. As a young mind, you have a fresh perspective of what the world needs and where it is going, so why not utilize that to create some cash flow? The invention or the business idea that you keep circling back to – focus on that, build on that, and reap the benefits once you succeed!

These are part of your options (to name a few) that can help you determine which professional path you want to take. After narrowing down your choice, we come to the next step of the planning process – finances!

## Financial Planning for Education and Scholarships

Fitting your professional future into your budget can sometimes mean making a little bit of a sacrifice. Since it is only for the duration you need to obtain the proper skills or degree, this should not be a problem. As a vibrant young teenager, you have plenty of options – if you don't have the necessary means to finance your next step it does not mean you should immediately quit!

All you need is a solid plan. So, here are a few resources that could get you started:

❖ See how you can save some money and make the most out of it. Check the available scholarships and whether you are eligible for any of them. As a student, many benefits and grants serve the purpose of helping you achieve your goals and dreams, so use them to the fullest extent!

✧ Create a balance between focusing on your education and your work (mostly if you want to do a good job at both). Many teenagers skip this step, firmly believing that they "got this." Well, do you? Set some time to think and create a plan that can help you achieve all the deadlines, finish all the work, and complete your goals. You can help prevent spiraling down into a hole filled with missed deadlines and opportunities.

✧ Be mindful that things can change in a minute. Understanding that there is a specific extent to which things can go one way if you don't maintain them is key. Upgrade your flexibility and remember to prepare yourself for everything. Because, as much as you give, sometimes, things can go awry. It is in those cases that you need to have a plan B, C, and all the other letters if you need to – make sure you are prepared for the unexpected.

✧ Always be on the lookout for new opportunities. Every new day is an opportunity in and of itself. As much as it sounds like a solid idea to make a financial plan, that does not mean that you should completely ignore some wonderful opportunities that may cross your path. Regularly check any resources that might be of help to you, and don't give up!

Create a stable financial structure that can support your next step in the educational process. Be mindful of those bad days, as they may come easily, but they may also go easily as well.

Now, we are at a crossroads – the subject of planning for your education and the training process to become a valuable part of the workforce is complete. But we are only getting started on the practical aspect of it!

The next chapter encompasses the power of practical experience. Learn all you can about it!

## CHAPTER 6

# GAINING PRACTICAL EXPERIENCE

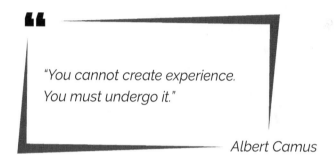

*"You cannot create experience.
You must undergo it."*

— *Albert Camus*

E xperience is not something that you can obtain by only listening to your classes or courses. For this bit, you need to dip your toes into the professional waters and find out how you can swim for yourself.

The teenage years are the best years of your life. But they are also the ones where you should work the hardest. In the beginning, it might seem like a waste of time to focus on gaining and sharpening your skills. But, if you look at the long run, you will soon notice how, with each passing day, you have a bigger need for them.

So, once you've established your plan for education and training, it is time to start gaining some practical experience. That will help you set a strong foundation for all professional curveballs that life throws at you later.

Do you know where to begin? Do you know your options? This is another confusing aspect on the road to finding the right career path. Thankfully, it is easy to overcome it! I have broken down the most popular choices for you below. Take a look at them and evaluate how they would fit into your situation – one of them will eventually work out for you!

## Volunteering, Internships and Part-Time Jobs

It is easy to become a part of the enchanted circle – you need the experience to get a job, but you need a job to get experience! I have noticed that this fact can create a bit of panic for some teenagers. No worries, there are always some pretty good options that can help you get started. As long as you are dedicated to your goal, you can achieve anything!

For a beginner such as yourself, it might confuse you to notice that plenty of job opportunities require a certain degree of relevant experience. This is a normal part of the job-seeking process, but when you are at such an early stage, how can you take control of the situation?

Well, there are many ways you can contribute to building your portfolio. For starters, take a look at the most common ones – volunteering, internships, and part-time jobs.

**Volunteering** – these are available in almost every field. In today's world, volunteering is the act of being an active participant in the community. When you start doing this at an early age, it sets you apart from the crowd and makes you more prepared for what's to come.

Consider this as an essential activity that will open the doors to finding the perfect job opportunities for you. Are you looking for some experience in the democracy field or maybe the veterinary field? A passionate individual like yourself should only view this as the essential steppingstone into the professional world. It will give you an insight into how your community works, bring some purpose to your life, and teach you some valuable lessons about work. Fun fact – volunteering can also improve your overall well-being and self-esteem!

Why not check out a few companies in your area? Do the proper research (depending on your field of interest) and note the few distinguished establishments you find. From this point on, all you need to do is get in touch with them and start volunteering!

**Internships** – some of you feel the need to benefit financially as well as professionally on the road to success. That is where internships come onto the scene. As with volunteering, you get to benefit from creating a wide network, get some experience, and help yourself learn about what you want to do later in life.

Even though remote work is becoming increasingly popular, as a teenager, you have more access to an internship than ever before. Think about dedicating a summer or a few hours of the week to this cause and see how it will benefit you in the long run.

After you have completed your internship in whichever field you like, (administration, social media, fashion, graphic design, etc.) you will come out the other end thriving! You might not notice, but through the process, you will not only gain a little bit of professional and financial stability but will also expand your theoretical knowledge beyond your wildest imagination. Plus, you get to amplify your resume!

***Part-time jobs*** – now, you are working toward getting a university degree, and that is your sole goal. So, why waste your energy with working a part-time job?

This is the mindset of a common teenager. You might feel like this would be an unnecessary distraction when in fact, it is the one thing you need! A part-time job can give you a unique insight into what makes the professional world go round. You will get to experience it for a short while and learn some valuable lessons during it.

If your soft skills are not up to par, you will certainly experience a revelation. Besides seeing how specific rules apply in the workplace, you will improve your time management, gain a sense of responsibility, and learn how to work in a team.

Last but not least, this will not only boost your resume but your confidence too!

Remember, these options are only the tip of the iceberg! There are as many options to gain experience as job choices, so buckle up because I have a lot more for you.

## Summer Programs and Camps

Now, while I was on the subject of internships, I mentioned that you can spend a summer learning and expanding your skills. If this is stuck in your mind, then this next part is for you.

First of all, let me applaud you for your good thinking! Considering a summer program or a camp is an excellent opportunity to grow, learn, and figure out what you want to do with your life. While many teenagers underestimate the subject of a summer camp, (sounds geeky at first) you saw the possibility of investing in yourself! At the end of the day, that is what matters the most!

On the other hand, if you are still on the fence or strongly against it, allow me to elaborate. What have your summers been like up until now? Going out with your friends, maybe reading a book, playing video games, and spending your time idly doing nothing important. If I am correct, then you probably need a change. As much as you deserve the break after 9 months of studying hard, there is a much better way to use your time and acquire something valuable.

To those of you that have not yet realized the benefits of investing in yourself over the summer, I dedicate this next bit to you:

- ✧ Start using everything you have learned so far – even if it has only been in theory, entering a summer program will give you the platform to try all you have learned so far. Whether it is a technical skill or a soft skill, this is the best place to see if it works, as it is a safe zone that will not lead to some serious repercussions.

- ✧ Go soft and go practical – you will be placed in a unique environment – a learning one. This is not only your time to shine but your time to also be a creator of a better self. Practicality is key here, so once you browse the plateau of available summer camps and programs, choose the one that will give you the best experience.

- ✧ It is about all kinds of skills – you may not have thought about this until now, but entering a summer program can help you plunge into a world without any kind of safety net. Deliberately place yourself in a position where it is obligatory to learn many life skills. It all starts from the smallest and simplest skills and builds up to the challenging ones you are looking to obtain. This can be a way for you to learn both how to make your bed and practice leadership skills. Sounds like something you'd want to experience, right?

✧ A summer program is not a place of anarchy – but a place of understanding and learning accountability. Yes, you will be left to your own devices, but you will be under the constant observation of professionals who know how to handle any situation. Consider them your mentors and let them guide you. These are usually a handful of counselors who are there for you to learn from them. They will hold you responsible for your actions to the fullest extent, thus giving you the trial, you need for a professional life.

✧ Learn without the stress of – school, exams, talking in front of your entire class – all of which can make you feel high levels of stress and anxiety. Everything changes the minute you are a teenager, so the important thing is to give yourself time to grow. But also, the space to grow. A summer program is a great way to learn without the added stress of classmates and grades. It is about letting go of your fears and fully committing to the tasks at hand.

✧ Make life-long connections – I know that expanding your network is the last thing on your mind when starting a summer program, but it is one of its most incredible benefits. When you look at it – both the counselors and your peers may end up being excellent and very valuable to you in the future – and vice versa!

I hope that I have helped you make up your mind on this one. Speaking of mind, this next one might be the perfect fit if you want to sharpen yours in a more competitive and challenging environment.

## Shadowing Professionals and Job Shadowing Opportunities

At this stage, you must wonder what various jobs look like. Is the stress level the same in any field? Is there a different level of responsibility depending on the type of work? Also, how do you know you have reached a stage where you are ready to become a professional or an expert in a particular field?

If there is one thing that can help answer all of these questions, it is a job shadowing opportunity. You are a teenager, which means that most of these vacancies where you can shadow someone are designed specifically for you.

Having this opportunity to shadow a professional means you get to have someone introduce you to the vast business world and what it encompasses. Additionally, it has proven to be a successful approach to bringing successful individuals into many fields, and it has become an acceptable – no, preferable course of action.

This can help you determine your major in college, realize what you want to do after you finish high school, and give you an idea of what the rest of your life would look like. Remember that question grown-ups always asked you? "What do you want to be when you grow up?" Well, after this, you should be able to answer it satisfactorily.

Do you know what you need to do to get there? Other than being polite and professional, you need to choose a company that can provide you with one of their employees as the best example of what you want to be. Request a shadowing appointment where you introduce yourself. Share your interests, which school you're attending, why you are interested in shadow work, and whether they have someone on the dates you're available. For this last one, keep in mind that not all will have someone available for the first dates you request, so showing some flexibility is a plus.

Once you make all the necessary arrangements, it is time to start the shadow work! It is key to realize that you are in the observer role and won't have much to do. In contrast, you will have much to see and learn. Even if you don't have any background in the field, use this as the groundwork upon which you will build a better understanding of the workplace as a definition.

There are many things you will learn on your job shadowing journey. The small tasks you get will result in you gaining the following:

**You will learn how the job you want works** – shadowing a professional will give you direct access to your future – you will see how you should function and witness a typical day that includes all the responsibilities, challenges, and issues.

**The connection with the other positions** – any job you choose to take up as a career path will have a close connection to another branch. With job shadowing, you will learn how to connect with various branches and form successful relationships. You will learn how to be a part of a well-oiled machine that works impeccably.

**Expand your network** – however long or short your shadowing experience may be, it is crucial to start networking. You are a teenager now, but the connections you coin will be the ones that can help you spread your wings in full glory once you become a part of the workforce.

**Learn how to learn** – don't be afraid to ask questions and take small matters into your own hands (when possible). This is how you can develop a more accurate representation of yourself and the job you want to do.

Note that, depending on the job shadowing program you find, the tasks may vary – substantially. Making the most out of it can only mean one thing – flexibility. Keep an open mind, whatever the situation, trust your gut, and think independently. Circumstances may change at any moment, so here are a few tips to help you out during those times:

- ✧ You don't need to focus so much on leaving a good impression, but you should always be polite and professional.

- ✧ Keep in mind that your mentor might have some demanding responsibilities and provide the space to finish them.

- ✧ Not everything will look interesting – a part of the experience may be incredibly dull – that is normal.

- ✧ Appreciate everything your mentor says to you – remember, they dedicate a valuable portion of their time to teaching you how things work.

- ✧ It is okay if, by the end of the shadowing process, you realize you don't want to pursue that particular career – consider it another lesson you have learned.

After you have gained all the necessary practical experience, you should be ready to write it all down – as a part of your resume! Do you think you got what it takes to create a successful one?

## Building a Portfolio or Resume to Showcase Skills and Experiences

It takes the skillful act of putting words together and doing it in a way that accentuates your capabilities to the fullest extent. However active you may have been with all the internships, volunteering, job shadowing, etc., you may not have the proper skills to put all your experiences into words.

More often than not, teenagers get confused when they come to this section, and not only because it poses quite a writing challenge, but many need to recognize the difference between a portfolio and a resume.

Before we go much further, help yourself – learn the difference.

**Portfolio** – the portfolio is a visual representation of your practical work. It should be filled with examples of your work. You might think that only photographers use a portfolio (due to the visual aspect of it), but anyone can use it. A portfolio can be filled with links, videos, texts, various illustrations, and so much more.

A typical portfolio includes an originality statement (a small paragraph where you write that the work included is yours and confidential). Furthermore, it should have a summary of your career, a brief biography, and a small paragraph that will serve its purpose as a belief statement. Here, you include your motivations, values, likes, and goals.

**Resume** – on the other hand, a resume is a more concise and less creative way of showing a company who you are. There are many formats for you to choose from, but all in all, it should contain the following – a summary of your working experience (as a beginner, you should list all the practical experience you have gained, including starting and finishing dates and contacts, in chronological order), add your education in chronological order too, and list all the skills you have (these include soft skills and technical ones, relevant for the position you are applying).

Before you start applying for the jobs you have found, you need to create an impeccable resume and portfolio that will set you apart from the crowd. There are a few ways how to do that:

**Research the role you're applying for** – there is nothing worse than giving your potential employer a bunch of information they're not interested in. Put some time and effort into researching the role you are going for and customize your resume to fit their needs (to a certain point). Remember, you still need to keep the information within reasonable and truthful boundaries.

**Add all your accomplishments** – gather all the recommendations, achievements, extra-curricular activities, internships, and programs you have undergone. Demonstrate to your future employer that your education and investment in yourself have been your primary goal up until then.

**Keep it short but include everything** – I know this sounds a little complicated, but you need to keep your sentences short. Include all the info you need, and especially for your resume. Keep it within a page.

**Promote yourself** – language is not the only thing that matters while creating your resume and portfolio. It is imperative to know how to promote yourself too, so further enhance it with color. You can even go as far as creating an online portfolio – that's always a showstopper!

By the end of this chapter, you've made it easier for yourself to become a person that has some participation in the practical section, not just the theoretical one.

As we close the chapter on gaining some practical experience, we open the next one – deciding what you want. Toward the end of the job shadowing part, I mentioned that you might not like what you see. Have you thought about what to do if that happens? Either way, see for yourself in the following chapter.

## CHAPTER 7

# MAKING INFORMED DECISIONS

> **"**
>
> *"Nothing is more difficult, and therefore more precious, than to be able to decide."*
>
> — *Napoleon Bonaparte*

N apoleon's decisions may not have always been right, but he is definitely right about this one. It is finally time for you to decide what you want. However scary it may sound, bear with me – there are ways to exclude your emotions and make a choice based solely on facts (ones you have gathered so far).

From knowing the current and future job opportunities to knowing how good or bad you would be at each of them, it is all about considering the info you have. That said, there are a few steps you can take that can help you pick a successful career alternative.

## Weighing the Pros and Cons of Different Career Options

You are a teenager, so don't be surprised if you find it very difficult to exclude emotions from your decision-making process. After all, this may be the most challenging step you face. Thinking logically, you must already have a few alternatives lined up, and now, all of them seem like good options! So, which one to go for?

Start enjoying the power of making a list with pros and cons. If you are unable to do it yourself, ask for help! Get your mentor, a friend, a relative – anyone whom you trust, to assist you. Making a decision this large requires your full attention and the need to analyze all the factors. I recommend you use all the deep research you have done so far, as well as some soul-searching.

It might be difficult at the moment, but *picture yourself ten years from now.* What do you see? Do you see a role where you can thrive and constantly move up the corporate ladder, or do you maybe see yourself as running your own business, making the rules as you go? Try answering this question truthfully – you will gain an excellent starting point for your career path.

You have a very big decision to make, so get your pen and paper out and start writing! Lay out all the options in front of you. Underneath each, make a division into two sections. One will be for the pros and the other one for the cons. Remember, you are making this decision based on your priorities and needs! Start writing things down. While you do that, do some further investigation of your own – down to the last detail! Take a look at the working hours, take a look at the experience needed for each field separately, and take a look at the benefits that are mostly offered for each position. Also, see if there is a possibility for growth in every field. As an inexperienced individual, you may overlook this, but some job positions can become generic over time. That being said, after a few years, you may find out there is no room to grow. It is much better to be aware of it before you are already deep into the work.

Consider this as one of the best aspects of your decision-making process. Right now, all opportunities may seem equal – when in fact, they are not. Instead of leaving it all to your gut, you are doing the right thing by filling out the negative and positive sides of every alternative you have.

In reality, when you look at the situation on paper, you will see that some concerns you thought were incredibly large can be handled in a minute. On the other side, you may uncover some potential opportunities or new concerns that will completely shift the focus of everything.

Trust the process – that is the most important thing to do. Find the thing that is the driving force that would pull you forward into professional success and discover what your breaking points are. For some, it might be the generic work I mentioned earlier. For others, it might be the long hours or maybe, the long commute. *For you, it will be anything that does not fit your wants and needs.*

The pros and cons list is just a plan where you prioritize your needs and goals and align them with the job opportunities on the market. I am explaining the market demand and how to understand it better below. Read it so you know how to make an even better and more informed decision.

## Understanding Market Demand and Job Prospects

As a teenager, you might not be able to identify what skills are necessary for the job market of today. During all this uncertainty, you might be panicking and unable to take a step in any direction. However, when your future employment is at stake, you need to understand both the market demand and the job prospects.

The uncertainty that is arising in the *market demand* at the moment is due to its dynamic nature. Things progress faster than usual, and it is all thanks to the help of technology. Many job opportunities considered solid and necessary about a decade or two ago are now slowly diminishing. Contrary to that, technology paves the way for many new prospects to emerge and promises these will be the exact ones that will lead society into the future.

What you might notice here is that the job prospects for you (based on the specific and soft skills you have) vary from the market demand.

*Let's talk a bit about disruptions.*

In a perfect world, as soon as you finish high school, go to university, and get a degree (or not), you start working within the field you want. Everyone gets the training and fulfills the requirements during high school, with almost no extra-curricular activities, and the transition from a schoolbook to an office desk is as seamless as possible.

In reality, things cannot be further from this. Nowadays, the world is facing a global skills gap since the market is constantly looking for a vaster skillset than anyone can achieve with traditional education. I cannot imagine how it is for a teenager such as yourself to face this kind of situation.

Fortunately, however limited your skillset is, understanding the market demand and looking into future job prospects can help place you a step ahead of everyone else.

Noticing a gap or a lot of inequalities between what you want to do, and your level of expertise is the first step in the right direction. This means that you have realistically evaluated the prospects and are ready to face whatever challenges may come your way.

You are now standing on the edge of a certain change. Instead of holding back and pushing your potential down, try doing the exact opposite. Embrace change, become change. The transition from studying to working can either make you or break you. Try to focus on the making bit.

Making yourself better for future *job prospects* comes from the ability to invest in your career development. That is what we have been learning about together until now, and that is what you will continue doing long after you read this book.

Do you need some tips to help you set up for the future? On top of all you have done until now, here are a few tips that can catapult you to the top of your employers' job lists!

**1st tip** – it is essential to stay on top of all the recent changes in your field of interest. All the recent changes equate to adding some new skills to your resume. As long as you are aware that change is constantly happening, you can stay on top of the situation and become a life-long learner. Consider this as a primary tip that will help you increase your employability. While you regularly update your skills, you will become more in sync with what employers want and what the market needs.

**2nd tip** – signaling that you are the best candidate for the job in any field requires having some professional validation beforehand. I have mentioned this many times before. Consider this as an extracurricular activity. Getting an extra certification or undergoing a seminar is somewhat of a precondition for entering the workforce. Many courses vary in importance, duration, etc., which can signal to employers you have taken the extra step to become eligible for a certain job position.

**3rd tip** – focus on positive development (and I don't mean this in the sense of making yourself presentable). Expand your views and interests as much as you can, and always have this in mind – *you are doing this for yourself.* Yes, showing a certain level of diversity is important, especially as a young person just entering the workforce. But at the end of the day, it is you who must be happy and fulfilled by it.

That leads me to the next aspect to consider – and that is the overall quality of life based on the career path you choose.

## Considering Lifestyle Factors and Work-Life Balance

Enough about technicality. Let's talk about practicality! By now, you must already have a system set in place and a certain lifestyle. You have your wants and needs, your goals, and your routines. You have your friends, your relatives, the people you are closest to. You have your hobbies and interests and things that help you pass the time. You have an entire life set up.

You have a certain lifestyle that, up until this point, has been supported by your parents/guardians. Suddenly, it is time to start thinking that you need to survive by yourself. It is time to let go of the training wheels.

Now, it is time to face the music and start thinking about how to make it on your own. Transitioning from a teenager to an adult feels like it's happening faster than a heartbeat. As soon as you turn 18, you're not a child anymore. On top of choosing a career path now, you also need to be extra careful about it so it can fit into your life and not change it as much.

Considering the balance between work and life is another one of the most important factors when choosing your preferred field of interest. It is not all about technical and soft skills and how to upgrade yourself. It is also about the overall quality of life and whether the subject you choose fits right into that.

If you are still looking at the pros and cons list you made earlier, remember to focus on choosing a career that helps you lead the life you want. Today, anyone, even a teenager, can notice that the lines between professional and personal life have become blurred, almost non-existent. The many trends, including flexible hours, working from home, being constantly available for work because of your smartphone, etc., have resulted in more of a negative response than a positive one. People who have been working for years have noticed how they bring their work home more frequently than before, and the shift in working hours is actually a shift in their entire day. That can lead to plenty of frustration and stress.

As a fresh mind who is only entering the world of work, remember that you have all the power to create the lifestyle that will suit you the best.

*It is important to maintain a balance between professional and personal life.*

*It is important to understand how valuable of an aspect this is.*

*It is important to strive toward creating a life for yourself that you like.*

I am hoping that I can help you reinforce this as soon as possible so you can enjoy the outcome for many years to come. If you weren't aware until now that life is full of choices, here it is. You are in front of one, a very important one. Any call you make   will influence your life.

There are a few perks that come with choosing to make a balance between your work and your personal life. Take a look at them below:

✧ You will have some time to focus on your physical health. It is important to maintain an active lifestyle, especially if the career path you choose tends to lead to a more sedentary lifestyle. Keeping your body active can help you remain focused, happier, healthier, and thus enjoy a good work-life balance.

✧ Never neglect mental health too. Being a workaholic may be a challenge for you now – you are young, full of energy, and have a lust for life. But what will happen in 10 or 20 years from now? Constantly focusing on your work without having time for yourself or your family and friends can result in a significant mental decline. You should be able to work without having any difficulties, so eliminate them from the start.

✧ There is a lot of stress in the world, don't let it consume you. Imagine taking up a career path that requires you to be available nonstop, gives you little to no freedom to do something for yourself, and makes you constantly feel under pressure. Eventually, you will start slipping, and you will be unable to manage your workload. Being under a lot of stress for a long period will only have a negative effect. This is why you need to opt for a job that teaches you how to manage your workload within working hours and allows you to leave something for tomorrow.

- ✧ When you have the time to focus on personal activities, you are more productive at work. This is a fact that you might not be aware of yet. Having some personal time for yourself, instead of only focusing on your professional engagements, can help you feel more fulfilled, thus be more productive and present while working.

All of this sounds excellent on paper, but once you are part of the real deal, it can significantly change your viewpoint. Sticking to a schedule you have set beforehand may be more difficult than you have imagined. It is at those times you should focus on the following:

- ✧ Start your work, and then set a goal. Try to be as realistic with your goals as possible. Understand that you can work both on a personal and a professional goal at the same time and make some room for both during the day. Doing this can help you maintain a better balance.

- ✧ While you work, work productively. Come to terms with the fact that you will only have a certain amount of time in the day dedicated to work, so make the most out of it. Increase your productivity levels by managing your workload and ensure that the extra tasks you may get from your work will not affect your personal life.

✧  This leads me to the following – separate state and church. Work is one thing, home is another, and while you are at home, refrain from using your work laptop or checking notifications after hours. If you want to maintain a balanced lifestyle, then stick to the schedule you've prepared for yourself.

✧  Last but not least, put stress management as your priority. Every job comes with its obstacles and challenges. Learn that while you're still a teenager. Also, find a healthy way that helps you cope with stress. It can be anything from taking a 5-minute break to developing a new hobby such as running, writing, listening to podcasts, etc.

Achieving a balance between work and life is essential. Instead of looking for a job that has long working hours, create stability by growing and enjoying more aspects of life than just the work one. Learn how to best evaluate where the biggest potential for growth is.

## Evaluating the Potential for Growth and Advancement in Chosen Fields

There is a sort of dramatic point to it all, but if you are not growing in life, then what are you doing exactly? The potential for career growth comes from the fact that you need a sense of purpose to start this journey. It is the path that separates you from the bigger picture and the career of your dreams.

Looking at that piece of paper with all you've written down on it. Can you easily spot the career paths where you'd have the biggest progress?

**Important note** – *career growth and career development are entirely different things. If we have focused on career development and transferable skills until now, career growth shifts the focus to entering a field that can help you thrive.*

Career growth has the option to advance in a particular field. In the long run, it helps you unlock a higher level of your potential, ultimately reaching the top! If you choose an area where, after a while, you will hit the ceiling of developing your skills and will start doing generic work, would that bring much satisfaction to your life? Contrary to that, choosing a field where one thing constantly changes will give you a plateau of options – ones you'll never be bored of.

After all, it is all about growth. Right now, the power is in your hands – you can shape your future life and add this secret ingredient in every aspect. You may not believe it, but in all cases, the possibility for career growth is the catapult that will move you forward. Essentially, it is highly beneficial to your well-being and will make you happy. So, choose career advancement, choose a better life, and choose yourself!

There is a balance in everything, isn't there? I applaud you for being able to stop and look within, weigh in all the factors, and make an informed decision. From all the steps we have gone through together, this might have easily been the most difficult one – so brava!

Consider this as a chapter where you need to take a breather from all you have done so far and rest your body for the next bit that is coming – taking some swift actions! We're going from a passive to an active exercise – let's see what you need to do there!

CHAPTER 8

# TAKING ACTION

> **"**
>
> *"Now is no time to think of what you do not have. Think of what you can do with what there is."*
>
> — *Ernest Hemingway*

I t is time to start acquiring the career of your dreams. You have done all this planning, researching, and investing in yourself. You are more than ready. You got this. These are the last steps you will take toward creating your bright future.

Taking action does not mean aimlessly running around and doing everything you can until "something sticks." It means being strategic about your future, striving toward the achievement of your goals, and of course, having a backup plan.

Are you excited to get started? Your own chapter in life is almost ready to unfold.

## Setting Short-Term and Long-Term Career Goals

There is a certain importance behind setting goals for yourself. It amplifies the importance of being a part of society, and for many teenagers, it gives the much-needed self-boost. Career goals are the motivation that can drive you forward and keep you jumping out of your bed, filled with excitement every morning.

You are a young person, so learning how to set goals properly is a skill you should possess. The trick to knowing what you want is being completely honest with yourself.

By learning how to set short-term and long-term goals, you create a mood board. Fill it up with everything you want to achieve.

It is important to note that it is not all about the destination. This is about the journey along the way as well. As a teenager, you need to stop to realize what resources you have at hand, determine that what you want to achieve is really your goal, not someone else's, and identify all the aspects where you might need some help. So, when you look at it, it is a simple thing to do. But it requires your full attention!

All of us have goals. They can be small, large, personal, or professional. Nevertheless, many teenagers confuse the action of setting a goal with the plan to achieve it. Daydreaming and thinking about what you want to achieve without doing anything about it will only get you somewhere, but not necessarily where you intended. It is a nice sentiment, though. Do you want to achieve everything you put your mind to? In that case, you need a solid plan to make it happen.

Actually, you need a **smart** plan to do it.

Are you wondering why the word smart is accentuated? SMART goals are a concept that can help you achieve wonders, especially with your career. It is the guidance many teenagers aren't aware of but find useful when they stumble upon it. This exercise can help you map out the steps to achieve your goal. It is probably one of the best exercises you will utilize, mainly because many people of all ages use it – constantly!

SMART is the acronym for the process you are about to undergo. Each letter represents a significant course of action you should take to achieve a successful career. Here is a short representation of what they mean:

S – stands for specific. By this point, you should have more than just an idea for your future self. Don't be afraid to go into a detailed plan – it might give you a clearer view of the big picture!

M – stands for measurable. This means tracking your progress. Take small steps toward achieving it, but ensure they are measurable. Take learning a new language as an example.

Dedicate an hour of your time every day to understanding it – that is a quantifiable way of achieving your goal.

A – stands for attainable. Be realistic with yourself. We have covered the aspects of what you can and can't do, underlining your strengths and weaknesses. Now it is time to use that. Don't push yourself too hard – instead, create an attainable goal (one you know you can achieve).

R – stands for realistic. Just like the previous letter, a realistic goal will help you develop your skills instead of creating a cloud of insecurities around you.

T – stands for time-bound. When you set up a goal, you should have a specific timeline. This means tracking down your progress until the process is complete. Breaking down the long-term goal into smaller milestones can help you prove there is constant progress and help you easily reach your goal.

You know what SMART goals are. Do you know how they support you? During the time you dedicate to fulfilling your dreams, this exercise provides you with some silent support along the way. Regard it as your fuel.

The process of setting a goal can have a positive impact on your overall lifestyle. After putting some time and effort into the plan, it can help you become better, stronger, and more successful. Ultimately SMART goals are shaping you into the person you want to be.

Take the lead as soon as you set your plan. Create some long-term or short-term career goals. As an exercise, it can provide you with many benefits, not only because it will give you the confidence you need (and open doors for you). Also, this is ultimately a rewarding experience. Working to achieve your dream results in picking up an extra skill or two on your way there. You will start feeling more independent and will learn from all the challenges you meet along the way.

Also, every time you set up a goal (be that a short-term or a long-term one), remember it can change at any time. Keep your mind flexible at all times. Give yourself a break every time you feel like you need one. Finally, don't forget to celebrate all the little milestones! It may seem insignificant, but success is made out of a lot of the small things you do every day. Pat yourself on the back after every milestone you achieve.

However, this is only the beginning. After all, you should know how to create a proper plan filled with strategies. For that matter, I will go over all the necessary details to do that in the following section.

## Creating a Strategic Action Plan

It is all about creating a professional development plan. Through this door, you will enter right into the professional world. Depending on your goal, you can outline some objectives. Create a solid plan on how to achieve them. There are numerous opportunities out there for you. You can dream of becoming an art director, a graphic designer, a party planner, someone who runs their own business, etc. You have so many available options; you just need to choose and start walking your path toward success.

That is what a strategic action plan is for.

The bottom line is - be aware of everything. When I say everything, I mean – start from yourself. Knowing where to begin means fully understanding what you are good at. This is your jumping point and the strength you hold when times get tough. There are a lot of factors that weigh in here. So, take a look at the outline I have prepared for you below – you might find it incredibly useful!

### Analyze Your Strengths and Weaknesses

We have mentioned them at the beginning, but as you can see, they are such an important part of creating a career path that we are constantly going back to them. Through them, you outline who you are.

As I pointed out before, these include both the soft and the technical skills you currently have. Once you finish evaluating yourself, you start outlining which ones you excel at, and which ones need improvement. The ones you are good at are the force driving you toward achieving anything you want. The ones that need improvement are the ones that are currently holding you back.

On the other hand, the list might lack a thing or two, so you might consider adding them and working on them – that's a great option too! Think skills, think traits. Any one of them can be polished to perfection through formal education or training. You may even achieve perfection by working on them without any help!

## *Write Down the Values*

As you start working toward making some progress on a professional level, you will see there will be many bumps in the road. Some are minor, such as tight deadlines or an argument with a colleague. But others are of a more considerable significance. These include when the workflow interferes with your decision-making process – when working under a lot of stress every day and doing a lot of work that you are maybe overqualified for, but without the proper compensation.

It is time to reconsider things when what you do interferes with your professional development plan. Before wasting 5 or 10 years at a job you don't like, outline your core values and find a workspace that aligns with that.

## *Think About the People Who Can Help*

When creating a strategic action plan, finding your weaknesses is an inevitable part of the process. Instead of letting it put you down, rise back up. I feel like there is no such thing as too much networking. It is essential to building your professional portfolio and ensuring you are noticed in the job market.

All the connections you can make with both offline and online networking can contribute to a flourishing career. Make it a part of your action plan to attend as many events and seminars as possible. Try to make a variety of it too – some of them can be events for improving your transferable skills, and others may be informal events where you reach out to people from your chosen industry.

Either way, the networking plan can be your ultimate jumping point to where you want to be.

### *Work on Your Image*

Another significant aspect of a successful career plan is presenting yourself in such a manner that employers can't say no to you. This means a presentable and decent style and having one all over your internet presence. Let's face it; everyone leaves a digital footprint, so make it count while you are working on yours!

What I mean is making sure your professional and personal online platforms are thriving. For example, create a LinkedIn profile, and showcase all the work you have done so far. Let future employers know that you are a dedicated and qualified individual.

Constantly add to your accomplishments. This includes everything from attending conferences and seminars to workshops and academies. In this way, you will demonstrate that you are dedicated to constant improvement.

### *Keep an Eye on Job Openings, and Don't Be Afraid to Make a Selection*

After all, you have come all this way and worked so hard on yourself – you should not allow yourself to be swayed into a job option that does not check all the boxes for you. Being flexible about it is one thing – completely changing your mindset, goals, and vision just to fit a profile is another thing. Appreciate all the work you've done so far and only consider possible employers who would do the same.

These are the handful of important things you should note when you are creating an action plan. Every step matters – so step into the land of opportunities with a solid plan.

At the end of the day, it is all about feeling capable and confident with who you are and confident with what you know. Once you reach that point, there is nothing you cannot overcome. The more honest you are, the more bullet-proof the career action plan you make will be.

## Overcoming Obstacles and Staying Motivated

Earlier in this chapter, I mentioned that sometimes, plans can change. The teenage years are filled with challenges and obstacles. These are an inevitable part of life. In fact, they complete life and give it fullness, representing the magnificent experience of being alive.

That often translates into the professional field. When you work on a goal for a longer time, you may get caught up in the process. That can ultimately bring some dissatisfaction and lack of motivation. It is a part of the journey. It can happen to anyone.

Do you notice this starting to happen to you? In the beginning, you were doing great, but something happened, and suddenly, you are feeling lost in the whirlwind of information and the next steps you're about to take. Suddenly it all seems like too much. Suddenly, you need some time to breathe.

Sometimes, when working toward a goal, you start struggling to find motivation right before you cross the finish line. The reality of the situation is that getting motivated is the most challenging part of the process. When you transition from high school into the real world – that is the biggest change. Being a teenager, you may feel like you don't have enough time to do everything in time.

Any transition process is difficult. Every action you will take in life may come with more than a few obstacles. If looking for the motivation to continue working on you seems too much, this section is designed especially for you.

Did you know you will come face-to-face with a few snags on your way to success? Did you know that about 80% of teenagers end up not following their primary career path? Something comes in their way of achieving their dreams, and they simply give up. That does not mean that they are unhappy with their current career paths. It only means they have encountered a change.

Whatever happens in your quest for the career of your dreams, you need to remain flexible and open to all possibilities. The process can be overwhelming but remember that it's not over until you get what you want and feel accomplished, happy, and satisfied with your choice. Curveballs will come and go, but instead of giving in to the pressure and the low motivation levels, try doing the opposite. Powering through is the best way to persevere.

Here are a few tips to help you get back on track.

Remember, it is all about finding the best approach for you. When you start feeling like your motivation levels are going down, it is time to switch it up. Don't be afraid of change – that only means that you are adapting and acknowledging yourself in all your glory!

## Learn to Remember Your Goal

There are so many things you need to do on your path to greatness. Starting with the big picture, then breaking it down into smaller bits, setting some short-term and long-term goals. You are constantly figuring out your next step – and that can be a lot. Any human could get caught up in the process and lose the necessary motivation to continue. When this happens, stop, take a minute to breathe. Remind yourself - what is your primary goal?

But try not to get too attached to the initial concept that you've developed. Also, do you repeat to yourself what you need to do every day? If you need to remind yourself what your daily goal is, is it the right choice for you?

### It is Okay if You Slip Up

As I mentioned, change can happen at any time. Once you are working on a long-term goal, it is natural for you to feel like your batteries are drained. Even if you miss a task or two, there is no need to be disappointed in yourself. The important thing is to get right back up and recommit to your goal. Did you manage to get off track because of your grades or a hobby? No worries, you got yourself!

Think about it this way – every person on the planet who had wanted to make a change eventually slipped. Everyone who has worked on themselves have had a minor or a major setback. Don't let that make you feel discouraged. Change and fluctuations are a natural part of the process – it means you are on the right path.

### Get Some Extra Support

Talk to your family, friends, or mentors and seek additional help. You would not believe how much of a difference a sound support system makes. Surround yourself with people who are familiar with your goals. These people would give anything to support you every step of the way.

This way, whenever you feel down or start feeling tired of pursuing your dream, you can turn to any one of them. Their job is to make you feel secure in yourself while reminding you to push your limits. They are here for you, so don't be afraid to share.

### *Visualization and a Positive Attitude*

This is the power couple you need to succeed! Start visualizing yourself – how you overcome any obstacle that comes your way, how you achieve your goal, and how that makes you feel. Use the happiness you feel each time you picture yourself succeeding and allow it to be the force that moves you every time you feel like stopping.

Positive self-talk can change a lot. It is not only an excellent way to keep your self-acceptance and self-motivation up. This practice also improves your overall attitude and mood. You deserve to achieve greatness, which is what you aim at – every day.

Embrace every barrier that comes your way. Refresh your memory – you are bigger than anything that stands in your way. Losing motivation can happen to anyone. Ultimately, your goal is a constant and positive change – and that doesn't come without a few challenges!

## Continual Learning and Adapting to Changing Career Landscapes

Adapting to change is just as important as overcoming obstacles. Another aspect that we have only touched upon is the subject of tomorrow. Every field – be it technology, biology, engineering, or writing – is led by experts, respectfully, and these people are improving the course of the future career paths of everyone that follows.

Right now, you are in the place of a follower – someone still learning and slowly applying the rules. Becoming a part of a workforce that is changing by the minute can feel like entering a race mid-way. Thankfully, this is not necessarily bound to happen – especially if you come prepared.

The key to becoming a part of the future is your mindset. Think as if you are already there. Up to this point, you have only been a high school student. Until you realize the best way to thrive is to become a lifelong learner, you might not get far with your career goals.

The ever-changing career landscape is what will nudge you in this direction – you weren't expecting this, right?

All of the skills that I have mentioned before are a great starting point. Your soft skills, such as time management, problem-solving, critical thinking, the ability to successfully communicate, etc., are the perfect ground upon which you will build yourself up. Combine that with the technical skills – but remember you constantly need to upgrade them too.

Ten years from now, you may have to face the fact that your career choice is now obsolete or a dying branch – what then? To avoid this from happening to you, choose a wide range of sources for improving and broadening your technical skills. If you allow this to become a continuous learning habit, you might end up as a part of a flourishing collaboration in a field you never even thought to be a part of.

Keeping an open mind when it comes to career searching can be a stretch for some, so here is a successful way to deal with it:

- ✧ Try to give some new skills a chance – you might end up liking them.

- ✧ As you do that, remember there is no need to try something extremely different from what you are doing at the moment. Be diverse but selective.

- ✧ Before entering the workforce, you have the unique position to look at things from a different perspective – from the outside. Analyze and look for weak spots – this is the commitment to lifelong learning.

- ✧ Once you become a part of the workforce, bring the outside – inside! Provide a unique point of view and help develop the creation of a steady stream of genius ideas.

Nobody can do this but you – you have the distinctive opportunity to rise to the occasion of always being a few steps ahead. Achieve that with the power of continual learning, and you will have no worries adapting to the ever-changing career landscapes.

Learning to recognize an opportunity is something you will practice for a lifetime. But, preparing to seize an opportunity you find is something you practice every day. By taking action and giving it your best to shape everything you have learned so far into an impressive representation of who you are, you will be ready to plunge deep into the next step of your life.

Finally, it is time to make the transition into the professional world. Don't worry. If you have done everything we have covered up until this point, you are more than prepared for it!

## CHAPTER 9

# TRANSITIONING TO THE WORLD OF WORK

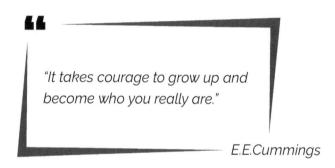

*"It takes courage to grow up and become who you really are."*

— *E.E.Cummings*

C ongratulations on reaching the final stage of this book! You are almost done with your secondary education, and it is time to turn over a new page! Now comes a time in your life when you will discover the endless possibilities of job professions.

Soon enough, you will have a crisp degree in your hand and a head filled with knowledge and useful information. After a successful secondary education, it is time to continue your learning process through another channel – work.

In this process, you become yourself. Now, learn how to utilize all available tools and make the most out of your working experience.

## Job Searching Techniques and Strategies

There is a difference in approach every time someone thinks of a job opportunity. Some people create opportunities and grasp them with both hands. Others have a more laid-back approach and wait to see when a new job opportunity opens up. Both methods are good, but it is time to think about which group you belong to more. Are you proactive about it or are you more passive?

My advice is – to be the former instead of the latter. Yes, you can still wait for an opportunity to open up, and you will meet it with arms wide open, but in the meantime, why not put some effort into it?

There are many aspects to consider as soon as you start looking for a job. Approach the situation from any angle – see that you have made the right connections. Make sure you've undergone all the extra training and academies, and mentally prepare for when that day comes – and you are employed.

I am talking about strategies and techniques. There are multiple ways of how you can approach the job market, and some of them are known to be very effective. As soon as you spot a job opening, thoroughly evaluate it before applying for it. For those who still need a nudge in the right direction, here is a detailed list of what you can do.

## 1. Make a Selection

Once you get out of school, you might become overwhelmed with all the possibilities out there. This is where you need to make a selection. Review all the open options and only apply to those that made the cut. How to make the proper selection? That's easy – all you need is to ensure the job opportunity aligns with your skills and interests.

## 2. Digital Footprint

The digital presence is the first thing your future employer will look at. Even though, for almost every vacancy out there, you need to send out a resume and a cover letter (sometimes even a portfolio), they are bound to Google you. Your online presence is what leaves a first impression long before they contact you for an interview.

Teenagers nowadays rule the social media platform, so why not use it to your advantage? Create a profile on a job-related social media platform (such as LinkedIn) and showcase yourself as a strong candidate.

You can even take an extra step. Depending on the field you are interested in, you can create your website and show your area of expertise. Think of it as the extracurricular activity that will set you apart. Through your digital footprint, you let your employer know your area of expertise, skillset, and work.

> A tip for those just entering the workforce: for example, if you are a graphic designer – pick a few subjects and make a few templates. This is a great way to show your abilities and provide the employer with a portfolio.

### 3. A Specific Set of Skills

The job you will apply for will require a specific set of skills. This is why you should constantly tailor your application. Many companies out there need a particular level of expertise and knowledge, so when applying, let them know you have it. Re-evaluate your skills each time and accentuate the ones that are of the most significant importance for the vacancy. Visit the company website and see what they focus on and what they promote. You may even find another opening for a job that suits you better!

### 4. Referrals Are a Power Tool

As long as you remember this, you are good to go! Until now, you must have done a plateau of extra activities, including internships or part-time jobs. Ask for a referral because you are more likely to get hired for the job of your dreams once your future employer sees that you have done very well before. You can even get a letter of recommendation. This is the additional step you take toward achieving your career goal. It works like a charm!

Making a career move can be easy if you know how to use all the tools at your disposal properly. And, while we are on the subject of tools, we talked about building your resume. Did you manage to create one that would capture the attention of your future employer?

If not, the next section is dedicated to all the details that make up a successful resume and cover letter.

## Crafting a Compelling Resume and Cover Letter

You may be good at many things, but writing is not one of them. The thought of sitting in front of your laptop and writing a resume and a cover letter scares you. Yet, you know that getting the job you want is right there at your fingertips. All you need to do is create a compelling cover letter and resume.

There is a certain importance to the application you send when applying for a job opening. These documents are a representation of who you are. Naturally, you want to make yours so good that they accentuate you as the best candidate. Every young professional should implement this. But gathering and writing down all your knowledge and qualifications is not enough.

So now, you sit in front of a blank page and ask yourself – how to create a successful professional resume that captures the essence of who I am?

Here is how.

**Resume** – it is a vessel through which you can prove you have the knowledge, skills, and expertise to tackle any challenge that comes your way. The moment you start writing your resume, you stop being a student and become a young professional. Present yourself in that light. Add all your relevant educational achievements to the position you are applying for (remember, I mentioned earlier that you need to tailor your application documents to the vacancy).

It is all about including relevant information. However, there are a few steps that are a must. Maximize the power of your resume by adding accurate information. Start by including your contact info (email, telephone number, etc.). Let your employers know that they can contact you at any time. Also, the beginning of a resume should include a summary. It can be short, only a few sentences, but make them count. Highlight your achievements that are related to the job you're applying for.

Working your way down, you should add your educational accomplishments (chronologically) and your work experience. The chronological order will reveal your age, so you can include any internships, part-time jobs, volunteering – anything you have done to accentuate your skills.

Next stop, you have the technical and transferable skills. Accentuate them. Let your future employer know you hold all relevant knowledge for the position. Use active language when describing your achievements and focus on important keywords. When tailoring your resume to a specific job, use concise language. Open their website and find a few keywords. Include them in your resume.

Prioritize the content that is relevant to the vacancy. You can exclude anything unrelated to the job you are applying for. Finally, proofread, and you're done!

**Cover letter** – the thing about a cover letter is that it should read like an essay, but it should be brief and to the point. A cover letter is not more than half a page, and it should speak directly to your employer about how your set of skills applies to the job you are applying for.

I advise you to avoid any fluff content. Instead of talking about what you want to achieve and how unique and original you are, talk about how you can use your skills to excel at the job. The cover letter should let your employer know you are a terrific hire. Here is how you can do that.

First off, you can use a cover letter template, but write a new cover letter each time you apply for a new job. Tailor it to the organization or company you're applying to and avoid being generic about it. At the very beginning, address the cover letter to the hiring manager. Using "to whom it may concern" or "dear Sir or Madam" does not show that you are very interested in the job, so avoid these salutations.

A good opening is everything. Make the hiring manager want to know more about you by hooking them from the first line of your cover letter. Make it snappy, passionate, and witty. Also, this is a great way to include the word "why." Why are you applying for the position? Why are you the best candidate? Let them know that you have a lot to bring to the table.

With the help of your qualifications and a few strategically placed examples, show why you are the perfect candidate for the job. This is the backbone of your resume. If you have a few experiences, accentuate the ones that present you the best.

Last but not least, finish off with a bang! The last paragraph of your cover letter is your last chance to make a memorable impression, so use it wisely. Sign off with a professional and positive attitude instead of loosely selling yourself. Create an appropriate closing, and hint to a CTA (call-to-action). Oh, don't forget to sign it with your first and last name too!

As with the resume, proofread it, make the necessary corrections, and you are done.

After you've successfully drafted and sent out your application documents, you come to the waiting period.

Depending on the company, this period varies from a few days to a few weeks.

This is your chance to prepare yourself for the interview.

## Navigating Job Interviews and Professional Etiquette

When the waiting period is over, and you get the call that you are invited for an interview is when it all suddenly becomes real. The interview is your chance to make a good impression and learn more about the company and its people. The interview's success depends on how you prepare for it, what you say during it, and what happens after the meeting. The three stages are essential to cover. On top of that, there is the factor of professional etiquette, so let's see how you can make the most out of it.

**The first stage** – the preparation stage is the process that will help you execute a flawless interview. You have a goal, and that is to show that you are the perfect applicant. Practice confidence, capability, modesty, and perseverance. Shift your focus from only leaving a good impression to presenting your true self in the best light possible. Come prepared because the interviewer can ask you some tricky questions. Know how to let them know your weak points but point out how you are working to improve them. Practice how to answer every question they have skillfully.

When I said to come prepared, that meant you should have a question for them too. Browse through their online presence and see what they are all about. If their vision and mission seem unclear, ask them what it is. It would help clear the air right from the start and leave a long-lasting impression that you are genuinely interested in the vacant position.

Work on your body language too. Remember to be polite with everyone you meet and have professional yet natural and open body language. Practice how to keep your back straight and your head up.

***The second stage*** – the second stage is what happens during the interview. Leaving a good impression is important, so I advise you to show up on time (that means at least 10 minutes early). Through this, you show your interviewer that you respect their time and appreciate the time they've taken from their busy schedule to fit you in. Let the professional attitude shine through, both inside and out. Dress appropriately, showing that you are ready for a successful start. Right before you enter the room, turn off your phone – you should have a smooth interview without any interruptions.

Take your portfolio with you (if needed). For those job options where you have to present a summary of your work, take your portfolio with you. It shows the recruiter that you are more than prepared. Use a pleasant and positive greeting and begin. During the course of the interview, be a good listener and answer all of their questions. Allow them to finish their trail of thought and show that you can be an excellent team player.

Table manners are everything, so if your employer is conducting an interview with you over a meal, then remember the basic table manners and refrain from any alcoholic beverages.

***The third stage*** – the interview is coming to a close, and everything went as smoothly as you expected. You have made an excellent connection with your interviewer, and now you want to express your gratitude for this opportunity. Follow up with an email and wrap up the entire experience with a positive attitude. Even though this is a small detail, it will make you more memorable than anyone else. On top of it, it says plenty about your personality and accentuates your attention to detail.

Having professional etiquette and working your way through a job interview takes a lot of work. There are many aspects to consider and look out for – curveballs are everywhere. Thankfully, with my help, you can easily overcome any challenge that stands in your way.

## Embracing Continuous Professional Development

Continuous work and self-development are the only ways to keep thriving in a constantly developing professional landscape. Things evolve as quickly as possible, leaving almost no chance for workers and employers to adapt. In such an environment, it is of absolute importance to keep refreshing your skillset and elevating your experience.

That is when Continuous Professional Development takes the floor. Also known as CPD. This is a program that is specifically designed to offer benefits to everyone who is a part of the workforce. As a young individual, fresh to the job market and ready to learn, CPD provides the best benefits to help you reach higher ground in your career. The best thing about it is that you can constantly upgrade yourself through the program!

The fast advancements in the professional world mean you should be ready to improve within minutes of entering the workforce. That is why you should focus a little bit on the CPD. Once you start taking an active part, you will see how your skillset will be constantly refreshed.

Do you know what you gain through a CPD? You put a little bit of effort and time into sharpening your skills, but you come out the other end like a winner! During a short period, you have the unique chance to work on specific skills you need to hone (or learn from scratch) and advance in your chosen field. Continuous professional development acts as a platform through which you are given a safe space to learn, develop, and improve.

The main goal of a CPD is gaining a wider palette of skill sets that will ensure the profession of your career. However, it comes with many other benefits.

✧ You keep up with the latest trends. There are constantly new trends out there, with the latest one being working from home. The norms change from one day to the next, thus creating the need to adapt. An increase in following the working trends has developed a sense of reason, community, and the demand for a CPD.

✧ You create a higher value for the profession. Take up a part in a CPD that is all about your profession and see how much you are missing out on. The constant development (especially if it is a field connected to technology) requires someone who keeps up – so be a step ahead!

✧ A boost in morale is always appreciated. CPD holds the power to make you more effective in the workplace. Through the program, you can open the door to career advancement and finally utilize your leadership skills.

✧ Refresh your memory as to why you chose this career in the first place. Even as a young person, you may find yourself in a dull position with only a few years of working experience under your belt. Enroll in a CPD program and refresh your interest in your role.

It is all about staying ahead of the curve and making yourself relevant. Enrolling in CPD programs and courses is the best way to do that. Look at it as the indispensable tool that will grow your career and expand it in every direction. Make yourself the best lifelong learner, unlock your hidden potential, and remain relevant in a dynamic environment.

A high level of responsibility comes with taking up a new job. Becoming a part of the workforce has never been easier and more challenging at the same time. But, despite that, you have grown so much and developed in unimaginative ways during these chapters. This was the final chapter – the cherry on top – that helped shape you into the strong professional of tomorrow!

# CONCLUSION

> "The only person who is educated
> is the one who has learned how
> to learn and change."
>
> *Carl Rogers*

C hange is an unavoidable part of life. It is the only constant thing in this life. My dear reader, my lovely teenager, you have come a long way since you started reading this book. Evolving from being a high school student to becoming an active participant in the community falls under the category of the largest shift in life – ever.

If you are still unaware of what you have done, why not look back and review the road you've traveled? After all, you have been focusing on completing the milestones one by one. Whenever this happens, every human is bound to pay attention to the task at hand, not noticing the change that happens all around.

As a teenager, so far, you have been exposed to a limited number of experiences. All of them have been great, and most have also provided a lesson you'll need in the future. But, after completing all the exercises we worked on together, you should have a clear path about how to proceed in life.

You started with your interests and your skills. You also unraveled some of the most important dilemmas of a teenager. It takes a lot of courage and self-reflection to find out the answers to questions about your future self. No wonder many of you may have even been scared about taking the next step of discovering yourself. Some of you may not have had any idea how to proceed. After all, preparing for your future career and exploring all the possibilities can be a confusing time. But thankfully, you have come out the other side shining through!

The most important thing you have extracted from your journey to discovering your future career path is reflection. Thinking twice before taking a step in any direction is better than aimlessly wandering back and forth. You learned how to harness and direct your energy toward something important to you, toward a field you'd thrive in.

Thanks to this book, you did not lose sight of all that is important to you.

Through careful planning and a few conveniently placed steps, you managed to build the future you. Now, who do you see when you look at yourself in the mirror? Do you see an accomplished individual ready to take on everyday challenges? Do you see a person who is more than capable of tackling a situation and completing tasks with flying colors? Here's to hoping for a positive answer, but either way, you have done an amazing job.

From reflecting upon your character, your strongest and weakest traits, to working toward creating a bulletproof resume, even to exploring the career options and researching the market of tomorrow – that is all you need to do to find out what you want to be.

But, most importantly, you learned two things.

The first one is pinpointing all the weaker spots using deep self-reflection. You have learned how to be honest with yourself because only a truthful approach can help you unlock your full potential. After making many lists with your interests, goals, and skills, you have learned how to differentiate them. Also, you learned how to rate them and how to improve them. You have even discovered the power of lifelong learning – something that can help you become a professional in any field you choose!

The second one is discovering what is good for you and properly researching the job market to get there. What you might not have been aware of up to this point is that exploring career options and analyzing the market in a way where it could provide some valuable information to you is difficult. Through this book, you learned how to do that with ease. Whether it was a traditional or a non-traditional approach, you marvelously tackled the act of gathering info on many industries. It is one of the greatest skills you will ever develop!

Remember, you did a lot of planning - and a lot of research too. You worked on yourself as hard as you could. Now, it is time to dive deep into the professional world.

There is one last lesson to be learned here. Throughout the book, I continuously mentioned that you need to put your dreams and needs first. Whichever path you choose to walk in life, make sure it is one you have chosen yourself. Even though you might need to manage your expectations as things unravel, I strongly advise you never to give up on your dreams.

Writing this book, even though it is filled with many logical steps and instructions, still has a very important undernote – believe in yourself and work to achieve your dreams! It would be my greatest pleasure if you use all the steps, I included here to get the career of your dreams. Manage your expectations but try to exceed them every time! At the end of the day, it is all about obtaining the career of your dreams! It is where you can make a difference! Become a part of a field that has always been your passion. That is why, throughout this book, I have constantly mentioned your beliefs and goals and their high significance. Because, in many ways, your uniqueness and all your talents make you a valuable part of this world. You need to utilize them to make the most out of it and bring some positive change into something important to you.

At last, you will feel a sense of completion – the work you've done to get to where you are right now is only a starting point, but it is still so much! Hopefully, I have helped you learn how to pursue whatever makes you feel satisfied and happy.

So go out there and start serving your purpose – I am confident you will always thrive.

# THANK YOU

Thank you so much for purchasing my book.

The marketplace is filled with dozens and dozens of other similar books but you took a chance and chose this one. And I hope it was well worth it.

So again, THANK YOU for getting this book and for making it all the way to the end.

Before you go, I wanted to ask you for one small favor.

**Could you please consider posting a review for my book on the platform? Posting a review is the best and easiest way to support the work of independent authors like me.**

Your feedback will help me to keep writing the kind of books that will help you get the results you want. It would mean a lot to me to hear from you.

## Leave a Review on Amazon US →

## Leave a Review on Amazon UK→

# ABOUT THE AUTHOR

Emily Carter is an author who loves helping teens with their biggest turning point in life, adulting. She grew up in New York and is happily married to her high school sweetheart. She also has two of her own children.

In her free time, Emily is an avid volunteer at a local food bank and enjoys hiking, traveling, and reading books on personal development. With over a decade of experience in the education and parenting field she has seen the difference that good parenting and the right tips can make in a teenager's life. She is now an aspiring writer through which she shares her insights and advice on raising happy, healthy, and resilient children, teens, and young adults.

Emily's own struggles with navigating adulthood and overcoming obstacles inspired her to write. She noticed a gap in education regarding teaching essential life skills to teens and young adults. She decided to write comprehensive guides covering everything from money and time management to job searching and communication skills. Emily hopes her book will empower teens and young adults to live their best lives and reach their full potential.

To find more of her books, visit her Amazon Author page at:

https://www.amazon.com/author/emily-carter

# REFERENCES

Boys & Girls Clubs of America. (2022, January 19). The Importance of Goal Setting for Teens. Great Futures. https://www.greatfutures. club/the-importance-of-goal-setting-for-teens/

Carlsson, A. (2023, June 16). Embracing Continuous Professional Development: Unlocking Career Growth and Success. LinkedIn. https://www.linkedin.com/pulse/embracing-continuous-professional-development-career-growth-carlsson/

Columbia University. Connecting Your Self-Knowledge to Career Options. Columbia University Center For Career Education. https://www. careereducation.columbia.edu/resources/connecting-your-self-knowledge-career-options

Columbia University. What to Know Before You Go: Researching Organizations. Columbia University Center For Career Education. https://www.careereducation.columbia.edu/resources/what-know-you-go-researching-organizations

Corhn, D. (2022, June 28). 5 Tips For Helping Teens Plan Ahead For A Sizzling Future Learning Coach Success. Connections Academy by Pearson. https://www.connectionsacademy.com/support/

resources/article/5-tips-for-helping-teens-plan-ahead-for-a-sizzling-future/

Crown copyright Province of Nova Scotia (2012, branding update 2015). Guide to Career    Planning With Your Teenager, Explore Careers Nova Scotia. https://explorecareers.novascotia.ca/sites/default/files/2018-06/16-44875%20Post-Secondary%20Guide%20Teenager%20English%20SPREADS%20FINAL-s_1.pdf

D'Monte, A. (2023, February 16). How Industry Mentors & Role Models Impact High School Students. LinkedIn. https://www.linkedin.com/pulse/how-industry-mentors-role-models-impact-high-school-students-d-monte/

Dr. Akos, P. (2020). STARTING EARLY: Career Development in the Early Grades Association for Career and Technical Education. School of Education, University of North Carolina at Chapel Hill. https://files.eric.ed.gov/fulltext/ED610366.pdf

Feder, M. (2022, August 26). 5 Steps to Making a Financial Plan for Your Education. University of Phoenix. https://www.phoenix.edu/blog/5-steps-to-making-a-financial-plan-for-your-education.html

Government of Alberta. (2023). Career Paths and Your Lifestyle. Alberta Alis, maintained by Alberta Seniors, Community and Social Services. https://alis.alberta.ca/look-for-work/career-paths-and-your-lifestyle/

INSIGHT REPORT MAY (2023, April 30). Future of Jobs Report 2023. World Economic Forum. https://www.weforum.org/reports/the-future-of-jobs-report-2023/

References

Kovacs, S. (2020, January 2). TEENAGE EQ AND ADAPTABILITY. Ambassador Leaders. https://ambassadorleaders.com/toolkit/eq-adaptability

Medically reviewed by: KidsHealth Behavioral Health Experts. Motivation and the Power of Not Giving Up. TeensHealth. https://kidshealth.org/en/teens/motivation.html

MIT. Network & Conduct Informational Interviews. Career Advising & Professional Development. https://capd.mit.edu/channels/network-conduct-informational-interview/

Page, M. team. (2021, November 16). Setting Personal Development Goals in 2022. Jobs and Recruitment Agency in Australia. Michael Page. https://www.michaelpage.com.au/advice/career-advice/career-progression/setting-personal-development-goals-2022

Pearson. (2020, December 10). Leading Students Through a Changing Career Landscape. Pearson. https://www.pearson.com/ped-blogs/blogs/2020/12/leading-students-through-changing-career-landscape.html

PWC, UNICEF, GENERATION UNLIMITED (2021, December). Reaching YES Addressing the Youth Employment and Skilling Challenge. Generation Unlimited. https://www.generationunlimited.org/reports/reaching-yes-addressing-youth-employment-and-skilling-challenge

Thompson, H. Make Your Action Plan. A Part of the Youth Advocates for Community Health Program. Community Youth Development Division of Extension. University of Wisconsin-Madison. https://youth.extension.wisc.edu/articles/make-your-action-plan/

U.S. DEPARTMENT OF LABOR. Soft Skills to Pay The Bills. United States Department of Labor. https://www.dol.gov/agencies/odep/program-areas/individuals/youth/transition/soft-skills

UNICEF (2022). The 12 Transferable Skills - UNICEF's Conceptual and Programmatic Framework. © United Nations Children's Fund. https://www.unicef.org/lac/media/32441/file/The%2012%20Transferable%20Skills.pdf

Made in United States
Troutdale, OR
07/30/2024

21655881R00089